PARANORMAL PARASITES

THE VORACIOUS APPETITES OF SOUL-SUCKING SUPERNATURAL ENTITIES

NICK REDFERN

AUTHOR OF *SHAPESHIFTERS*

Llewellyn Worldwide
Woodbury, Minnesota

Paranormal Parasites: The Voracious Appetites of Soul-Sucking Supernatural Entities © 2018 by Nick Redfern. All rights reserved. No part of this book may be used or reproduced in any manner whatsoever, including internet usage, without written permission from Llewellyn Publications, except in the case of brief quotations embodied in critical articles and reviews.

FIRST EDITION
Second Printing, 2021

Book design by Bob Gaul
Cover design by Kevin R. Brown
Cover illustration by Dominick Finelle/The July Group
Editing by Annie Burdick

Llewellyn Publications is a registered trademark of Llewellyn Worldwide Ltd.

Library of Congress Cataloging-in-Publication Data (Pending)
ISBN: 978-0-7387-5355-3

Llewellyn Worldwide Ltd. does not participate in, endorse, or have any authority or responsibility concerning private business transactions between our authors and the public.

All mail addressed to the author is forwarded, but the publisher cannot, unless specifically instructed by the author, give out an address or phone number.

Any internet references contained in this work are current at publication time, but the publisher cannot guarantee that a specific location will continue to be maintained. Please refer to the publisher's website for links to authors' websites and other sources.

Llewellyn Publications
A Division of Llewellyn Worldwide Ltd.
2143 Wooddale Drive
Woodbury, MN 55125-2989
www.llewellyn.com

Printed in the United States of America

CONTENTS

Introduction 1

1: Supernatural Energy 5

2: Lovers' Lane Beasts 21

3: Black-Eyed Children 35

4: Shadow People 47

5: Hungry Ghosts 55

6: Bloodsuckers 67

7: Mind Monsters 85

8: The Djinn 97

9: Soul Stealers   107

10: Aliens and Abductions   125

11: Creatures That Make Us Sick   139

12: Bedroom Invaders   149

13: Monsters of a Mysterious Island   165

14: Bigfoot   177

15: Zombies   189

16: Energy Suckers   195

Conclusion   211

Bibliography   217

Acknowledgments   235

INTRODUCTION

The world around us is not as it appears to be. In fact, far from it. As we go about our daily business, working and living our lives, something dark and dangerous is taking place behind the scenes, and it has been going on since the dawn of civilization. Most people remain oblivious to the truth and don't even realize it. Now and again, however, someone will stumble upon the startling reality that potentially affects and dictates the lives of just about all of us.

What am I talking about?

Nothing less than a monstrous collection of supernatural entities that terrify and torment us, and have done so for millennia. They do far more than that, however. They feed upon us. Like bloated, paranormal leeches, they suck us dry as they seek to fuel themselves with our psychic energy, high states of emotion, sexual energy, and human life force.

They hate and despise us, but, paradoxically, they cannot live without us.

Extensive data exists that strongly suggests that the human soul, essence, or life force is something that all of these entities—the vast majority of which exist in states of pure energy, but can take on just about any form they choose—need to survive. Have you ever woken up, drained and utterly exhausted, from a terrifying nightmare that didn't seem like just another regular dream? If the answer is yes, you may have been fed upon by these infernal things. When we sleep, we are at our most vulnerable. And that's exactly how they want us. A dream is not always a dream, as strange as that might sound. Sometimes it's an indication that, as you sleep, and as your guard is down, these voraciously hungry monsters are, in essence, eating you.

Among these creatures are the Shadow People: hostile things that typically manifest between 1:00 and 4:00 a.m., and who have the ability to paralyze us and drain our bodies of energy in much the same way that the vampires of folklore would drain people of blood. In fact, as this book shows, such distorted tales of vampirism almost certainly had their origins in the worlds and actions of these multidimensional things.

Equally dangerous are what can accurately be termed *supernatural seducers*: dangerous entities that thrive on sexual energy—for example, orgone energy, as theorized and documented by Wilhelm Reich. A highly charged, sexual dream may be deliberately initiated by such things, which, over the centuries, have been referred to as incubus, succubus, Lilith, and the Old Hag. This may also be why so many supernatural encounters occur at so-called "Lovers' Lane" locations. In these cases, voyeurism and sexual emotion lead to feeding.

Poltergeists—violent entities that can cause chaos in the home and delight in tormenting us as much as they are energized by us—are also part of the equation, as are thought-forms and tulpas. These are creatures created within the human mind and the depths of our imaginations that can be externalized and given a strange form of life in the real world. Key to the survival of tulpas and thought-forms is that we believe in them. The stronger our belief, the greater the ability of the tulpas to survive. In other words, they feed on—and coldly and carefully nurture—our belief systems.

For example, there is the Slenderman, a sinister figure that started out as an internet experiment, but has mutated drastically in the last few years, to the extent that numerous people report having seen the Slenderman in the real world. It's a perfect example of a modern-day tulpa or thought-form running wild in our reality. Witnesses describe seeing the scrawny, black-suited figure looming over their beds in the dead of night, extracting energy and dining in a fashion that would have chilled even the likes of H. P. Lovecraft and Edgar Allan Poe.

The Men in Black (MIB) fall into this category, too. Those who have had UFO encounters and have been visited by the pale-faced ghouls known as MIB state that while being threatened and intimidated by the MIB they have felt cold, clammy, weak, and lightheaded. As many of the unfortunate witnesses have stated, it's as if the MIB are draining them in the same way that a flashlight drains a battery. And, using the same analogy, when the light finally goes out, we do too.

Now, it's time to take an in-depth look at all of the above entities—and various other supernatural creatures—that see us as nourishment and nothing else. The list includes hungry ghosts; the extraterrestrial Greys of ufology; terrifying reptilian creatures that are also a part of UFO lore; the monsters that inspired Bram Stoker to write his classic; gothic novel, *Dracula*; and supernatural cats that—according to ancient lore—steal our breath as we sleep.

The stark and terrifying truth is that the earth is one big farm. And for these energy-based entities … we are the cattle.

Note: At their request, the names of some of the people referenced or quoted in the pages of this book have been changed.

1
SUPERNATURAL ENERGY

Before we get to the issue of what types of supernatural entities are using us as a source of food, it's first very important to understand the nature of the kinds of energies that are being reaped from us on a massive, nearly never-ending scale. Yes, some such entities feed on us in the conventional sense—by literally killing and eating us, as you will later see. The majority, however, do so in a stealthy, camouflaged fashion, essentially so that we don't get a full understanding of what is afoot in our world.

We'll begin with the phenomenon of prana. Satyananda Saraswati, born in India in 1923, was a teacher of yoga and the author of dozens of books, including *Kundalini Tantra*, *Yoga Nidra*, and *Sure Ways to Self-Realization*. And, as a swami, he was a teacher of Hinduism. Saraswati, who died in 2009, said the following about prana in 1981, which is reproduced in an online article titled "Prana: the Universal Life Force":

> In the physical body we have two types of energies. One is known as prana and the other is known as mind or consciousness. That means, in every organ of the body there should be two channels supplying energy. Modern physiology describes two types of nervous systems—the sympathetic and the parasympathetic, and these two nervous systems are interconnected in each and every organ of the body. In the same way, every organ is supplied with the energy of prana and the energy of mind.

It's no wonder, then, that *prana* translates into English as "life force." That's exactly what it is. But it's far more than that. Hindus believe that prana is the key to having a long and healthy life. That certainly applies to Saraswati, who was pushing ninety when he died.

Five Energies We Cannot Live Without

It should be noted that there are five degrees of prana. Prana itself is responsible for ensuring that our oxygen levels meet the requirements for a healthy body, mind, and attitude, as the Yoga in Daily Life website notes, in an article titled "Prana."

Vyana has a major effect on our minds and our emotional states. When we are depleted of vyana to an unhealthy degree, Hinduism tells us we are in deep danger of descending into states of turmoil: panic attacks, depression, stress, serious sleeplessness, complete nervous collapses, and even the likes of bulimia and anorexia—both of which can be made much worse by stressful situations. Vyana also helps to aid circulation in the human body, something that can help to keep things like heart attacks at bay.

Apana is noted for the fact that it takes care of the body, from just above the waist down to the toes. If apana is lacking, or has been taken by a parasitic entity of supernatural proportions, a person can find themselves blighted by all manner of conditions, such as kidney stones, circulation problems in the legs, and stomach-based ailments like colitis and ulcers. Constipation, diarrhea, and problems passing water can all occur when apana is not at the level that it should be.

Samana is, without a doubt, one of the most important of all the energies that Hinduism tells us are vital to a healthy and vibrant life. It plays a significant role in the matter of food. In today's world of fast food, junk food, cakes, candy, caffeine, too much soda, and a lack of exercise, it's no wonder that large numbers of people are falling victim to the likes of diabetes, heart disease, strokes, and other ailments that could be avoided if people would look after themselves.

Samana performs a vital role, in the sense that it is responsible for the way in which energies derived from food are circulated and digested. The problem is that when we are eating nothing but junk, there is very little for samana to make use of in a positive way. Those who adhere to the idea that samana can have a major effect on our bodies—and as a direct result of what we put in it—advise us that a vegetarian lifestyle is a good way to go, and may help keep such conditions as heart attacks and diabetes at bay.

Finally, we have udana, which is inextricably linked to matters of a psychic and supernatural nature. Udana sends powerful energy from one of the human body's most vital organs, the heart, to the brain. In doing so, udana allows a person to become more and more psychically aware—if, that is, one adheres to a lifestyle that also sees the other four forms of prana working to their maximum potentials. It is said that those who work deeply with udana energy can develop the uncanny ability to defy gravity—in other words, to levitate. Udana, in high levels, also permits a person to control the means by which their soul can travel—in an astral, disembodied form—into other realms and higher dimensions of reality. Kundalini, an energy at the base of the spine that provokes enlightenment of the supernatural type, also benefits greatly from high levels of udana.

Healing Via Energy

It's important to note that prana is not just an energy that can have a major impact on the human mind and body; it is also something that can be used to heal the sick. Those of the Hindu faith who are skilled in the field of "pranic healing" believe that such healing can help a sick person in an astonishingly large number of ways, regardless of whether the sickness is in the mind or the body, or even both. Although the process is steeped in mystery, it can be explained in simple terms. Pranic healing involves the removal of bad, negative, and diseased energies from the body. The healer then floods the affected person's body with new, uncorrupted energy. To say that it mirrors the process of changing the oil in our cars every few months would not be too far wide of the mark.

Conditions that respond very well to pranic healing include chronic migraines, colds, digestive issues, both high and low blood pressure, heart palpitations provoked by anxiety, obsessive-compulsive disorder, agoraphobia, claustrophobia, and depression. When the five pranas are fine-tuned by the healer, and are finally in perfect sync with one another, the person being helped is well on the way to making a good recovery. It's also important to note, though, that following a lifestyle in which prana plays a huge role is not meant for someone who can't fully commit to it. It's very much a lifestyle that has to be practiced for one's entire life. Food, drink, mindset, and physical condition all come into play—and all will have a bearing on health. Or, on the lack of it.

Because of the level of positive effects prana has on the human body, it's hardly surprising that paranormal creatures, which endlessly require powerful energies to survive, would target our prana and quickly reap it for their own purposes and needs. For them, it's the equivalent of winning the lottery. You'll soon come to see that many of the conditions that dangerously lowered levels of prana can cause or make worse—such as psychological illness, ulcers, and significant weight loss—have all been reported in cases referenced in this very book.

By trying to maintain our prana energy levels to the highest degree possible, we might at least be able to keep the side effects of depletion to a minimum. In turn, that may give us the strength to fight against the paranormal invaders and keep them at bay. Shielding ourselves with prana—as an ancient knight might with a suit of armor—is something we should all consider doing.

Sexual Energy

Paranormal encounters that have a significant sexual aspect attached to them are highly common, and particularly those cases that involve the depletion of human energy by supernatural creatures. From the incubus, the succubus, and Lilith of millennia ago, right up to today's encounters in Lovers' Lane locations, the angle of sex is ever-present—as you will come learn. But what, exactly, is the connection? The answer to that important question lies in the work of Dr. Wilhelm Reich and his research into what he termed "orgone" energy. Reich's work was truly groundbreaking and, today, provides a strong and logical explanation for how and why supernatural entities are so reliant on us, from the perspective of sucking in sexual energy. From the days of the monsters of Sumerian culture to the present era, it is orgone on which so many of our monsters feed. But before we get to the issue of this mysterious energy itself, let's first take a look at the life, work, and ultimately untimely death of the man who uncovered and named it.

Wilhelm Reich entered this world in 1897, specifically on March 24. The location? Dobrianychi, Galicia, in central-eastern Europe, although German-speaking Reich was a citizen of Austria until the age of forty. After the age of forty, Reich fled to Norway, where he taught in Oslo. He then moved to the United States in 1940.

By all accounts, Reich's fascination with science and technology went right back to the early days of his childhood. Even by the age of just eight, he had his very own lab in which he bred numerous different kinds of insects. Reich was fascinated by the reproductive processes of such creatures, something that most assuredly had an impact on his interest—later in life—in human sexuality and reproduction.

Reich benefited from the fact that he was homeschooled, something that allowed him to focus more on the things he wanted to learn, rather than on things in which he had no interest. Reich's childhood was not without its turbulent times though; his mother, Cecilia, killed herself when Reich was just thirteen. At the time, Cecilia was having an affair with one of Reich's tutors and young Wilhelm found out about it. For a while, he said nothing. He was, however, in an undeniable state of conflict: Should he remain silent or tell his father, Leon? The day came when Reich chose the latter option. Cecilia, devastated that the truth of her affair had gotten out, took her own life—which Reich partly blamed himself for, and which he never really got over. There was more devastation for Reich, too.

From Europe to the United States

In 1914, when the First World War erupted and spread across Europe, Reich was forced to make a hasty exit from his hometown—it was either that or risk falling into the hands of hordes of Russian soldiers. There was no alternative. Reich hit the road and he didn't look back. He was no coward, though; he fought valiantly in Italy and reached the rank of lieutenant. Things didn't get any better. While fighting in the war, Reich learned to his shock that his father had passed away in 1917 from the effects of tuberculosis. Realizing that his old life was now completely gone—as, also, were both of his parents—Reich elected to find a new life for himself. He certainly achieved that and much more.

With the war finally over in 1918, Reich decided that education was the road he wanted to take, and he enrolled at the University of Vienna, focusing specifically on medicine. By all accounts, Reich was an excellent student; in 1922, he graduated and secured an MD degree. From there, it was almost like the sky was his limit. After receiving his degree, Reich continued his work, this time at the Neurological and Psychiatric University Clinic.

In addition, in 1919, Reich came to know none other than the acclaimed Austrian neurologist Sigmund Freud. They had a mutual interest in the study of human sexuality. In fact, Freud viewed Reich's work in the field of sex and psychoanalysis of such importance that he offered Reich the position of deputy director of his clinic, the Vienna Ambulatorium. Reich continued to work in Vienna through 1930, after which he spent time in Sweden, Germany, and Denmark. That was followed by five years in Norway. It was the rise of Adolf Hitler—and his increasing aggression, which ultimately led to the outbreak of the Second World War in September 1939—that saw Reich head for new pastures, specifically the United States.

Defining Orgone, the Ultimate Sexual Energy

Reich was fortunate enough to be issued a visa to allow him entry into the United States in August 1939—just a couple of weeks before war with Hitler began. For the next two years he was employed at the Lower Manhattan–based New School, where Reich's interest in alternative medicine, sex, and psychoanalysis increased. It was his research into what one might call a supernatural form of energy that really put Reich on the map. One could also say that it led to his downfall and, ultimately, to his death. But let's not get too far ahead of ourselves.

As far back as the 1930s, Reich had researched what he ultimately came to call *orgone*, or *orgone energy*. In a 2013 article titled "Understanding the Life Force Energy That Charges Us All: Orgone Energy & the Orgone Accumulator," Mark Denicola wrote: "Orgone energy, a term coined by Reich himself, is best described as a life force energy that can be found everywhere, even on the surface of the earth. This energy, Reich believed, was capable of healing the sick, optimizing body function and even adjusting weather formation."

An important question is this: how did Reich reach this particular conclusion? The answer is both simple and controversial. Reich used both male and female volunteers to monitor their levels of electricity when their genitals were stimulated. Because our bodies are made up of atoms, we are able to produce electricity. By comparing those volunteers with people in nonaroused states, Reich noted something amazing: that not just sex itself, but sexual arousal and fantasizing also led to profound increases in energy levels. Or, as Reich himself worded it, "a bio-electrical discharge," which he concluded was present in all living organisms. It became famously known as orgone, which was derived directly from the word "orgasm."

Dr. Paul Chambers, in his 1999 book *Sex & the Paranormal*, stated: "Sexual arousal, said Reich, was like a thunderstorm, with the orgasm being like a lightning strike, discharging all the built-up sexual energy from the body."

There was far more to Reich's work, too. As well as digging deep into the mysteries of orgone, Reich also started focusing on yet another energy-based phenomenon. He called them "bions." They were, Reich concluded, infinitely small sacs of energy that could morph into one-celled entities. Reich said there were two kinds of bions: the reds and the blues. Incredibly, Reich claimed to be able to see the two groups of bions essentially "fighting" each other when placed under a microscope. This was yet another breakthrough for Reich, one that further bolstered his belief that energy was extremely misunderstood—and Reich saw himself as the man who was going to find the truth.

Reich Accumulates Orgone

Reich went on to assemble what he called an "orgone energy field matter." He claimed it could measure orgone levels in a person—and that he was able to determine the huge fluctuations between someone in a relaxed state and someone else in a highly sexual state. Next on the list was the unveiling of Reich's "orgone energy accumulator." It can best be described as a large wooden box, which his volunteers sat in. The outside of the orgone energy accumulator would be coated with organic materials; the interior, however, was made of metal. Reich believed that orgone would be attracted to the external side, and would then radiate within the box, thus bathing the person in orgone and increasing their energy levels. The more he dug into his orgone-based research, the more Reich came to believe that orgone had the potential ability to cure some of the most serious conditions on the planet, including cancer and psychological conditions such as sexual anxieties, neuroses, and much more. Reich's work attracted the attention of numerous famous people in the field of the arts, including Jack Kerouac, William S. Burroughs, and J. D. Salinger.

Because Reich concluded that orgone had an attraction to and an affinity for water, he was led to believe he could use targeted orgone to manipulate the weather, too. In other words, complete weather control. Powerful winds, storms, deluges, thunder, and lightning: Reich saw himself as the man who could command them all. It was not destined to be, however.

The Government Steps In and Reich Goes to Prison

Although the US Food and Drug Administration (FDA) took a decidedly dim view of Reich's work and his alternative theories, he certainly had a massive group of followers. All of them felt that the sexual energy known as orgone was, essentially, the equivalent of a huge, powerful battery that could both energize and revitalize. Throughout the late-1940s and into the mid-1950s, Reich was someone many people listened to—and they listened very carefully. Between 1948 and the time of his death just under a decade later, Reich wrote many successful books, including: *Ether, God & Devil*; *Cosmic Superimposition*; *The Invasion of Compulsory Sex-Morality*; and *People in Trouble*.

Eventually, for the FDA, enough was most definitely enough. Reich's real troubles began in February 1954 when the US Attorney for the District of Maine sought an injunction to prevent Reich from selling his accumulators outside of his home state. It worked, although Reich could not have cared less. He continued to sell them, government be damned. Then, in May 1956, Reich found himself in majorly hot water when an employee of the FDA posed as someone wanting an accumulator of their very own ... and they conveniently wanted it shipped out of state. Reich was delighted to oblige—until, that is, the truth behind the FDA's ruse hit him squarely in the face. He was busted. Most disturbing of all, a number of Reich's books were quickly withdrawn from availability by the government. And, shortly afterward, hundreds of copies of his titles were not just confiscated, but *burned*. To say that it was a definitive witch hunt would not be far off the mark.

One month later, the FDA descended on Reich's labs and ordered that his accumulators be destroyed. There was very little that Reich could do to prevent such a thing from happening. Then, in August 1956, no less than *six tons* of Reich's materials—his journals, the remaining copies of his books, and his mass of equipment—were ordered to be destroyed, in what turned out to be a blazing inferno. Following that, there was the not insignificant matter of a two-year prison sentence for what the US government perceived as Reich having sold bogus technologies. Reich didn't last long, though: he was found dead on November 3, 1957, in the Lewisburg Federal Penitentiary in Pennsylvania. The verdict was heart failure. He was just sixty.

There are indications that even today the government has its uneasy concerns about Reich and his work. In 1999, the FBI placed almost eight hundred pages of previously classified files on Reich into the public domain. The documents were soon uploaded to the FBI's website. Eight years later, however, the documents were quietly removed. The file continues to remain absent from its original website, as well as from the FBI's additional site, The Vault, which was created in 2011. The FBI states that the file was removed as it was not seen as being historically valuable. Reich's followers would certainly disagree with that conclusion. Fortunately, the FBI's file on Reich can still be found online—at archive .org—under the title "Wilhelm Reich: Federal Bureau of Investigation."

As for Reich's almost legendary orgone, even though US authorities had no time for it and did all they could to shut Reich's work down—and succeeded in doing so—it's an important part of the story of paranormal parasites in our midst. In fact, it's a vital component of the overall controversy. As we have seen, Reich concluded that orgone was a form of sexual energy that acted as a battery. Orgone could be directed into a person and offer them a new life, one filled with vigor and absent of anxieties. More importantly, though, orgone could be *removed* from the body—basically the equivalent of putting the accumulator in reverse.

There is very little doubt that this is what so many people have experienced for millennia and continue to experience now. Lilith, the incubus, the succubus, the Old Hag, and the horned Goat-Man are entities you will soon become acquainted with. They all have two things in common: they are attracted to human sexuality and they have the ability to drain us of our vital energies.

Having addressed the issue of the kinds of energy that supernatural monsters feed on, let's now take a look at those dangerous creatures that seek to devour us.

2
LOVERS' LANE BEASTS

There is perhaps no better and more relevant example of how orgone energy is regularly being depleted from our bodies by paranormal entities than what I call the "Lovers' Lane phenomenon." From all across the world there are countless tales of paranormal activity occurring in places where "courting couples" hang out late on dark weekend nights. And many of those tales have at their heart such beasts as Mothman and Bigfoot—which suggests they too are paranormal parasites, and not the wholly flesh and blood animals that so many people assume them to be. UFOs also come into play in this issue too, as we shall soon see. But we'll begin with the aforementioned Bigfoot.

Sasquatch and Sex

Texas may not be the first place most people think of when the issue of Bigfoot surfaces. The vast majority of us would very likely equate the creature with the massive forests of the Pacific Northwest. But the eastern portion of Texas is heavily forested too—particularly as one gets closer and closer to the border with Louisiana. One place with a long history of Bigfoot activity is the Big Thicket—a massive area of extremely dense and mysterious woodland that spans more than 113,000 acres—which is not at all far from the city of Houston. In May 2014, the online *Houstonia* magazine interviewed the now-late Rob Riggs, who spent years investigating Bigfoot reports in the area, which he compiled in his 2001 book *In the Big Thicket: On the Trail of the Wild Man*. The article was appropriately titled "Bigfoot Is Hiding in the Big Thicket."

During the course of the interview with Riggs—which was done by journalist Michael Hardy for this article—interesting stories came out:

> When Riggs ran a notice in the paper calling for stories of unusual sightings in the woods, he was deluged with letters. A teenage girl claimed that a giant ape had chased her away from a cemetery. A couple in a car on Ghost Road—the local lovers' lane—reported that Bigfoot jumped on their hood, forcing the man, who fortunately had his shotgun handy, to scare the creature away by firing at it through the front windshield.

I got to know Riggs well after we first met in 2003, and he told me that Lovers' Lane–style encounters amounted to an integral part of the overall Big Thicket–based Bigfoot phenomenon. While Riggs, in the earliest years of his research, was of the opinion that the creatures were unknown apes and nothing else, by the time his *In the Big Thicket* book was published, he was sure there was a supernatural component to it all. Riggs was clearly not wrong, as the evidence shows.

Beware of the Beast of Bolam

In the latter part of 2002 and into the early months of 2003, the UK was inundated with reports of Bigfoot-type beasts. From the southernmost parts of England to practically the northern tip of Scotland, people claimed to have had encounters with large, hair-covered man-beasts—many of a marauding and violent kind. One of those who was determined to get to the bottom of the mystery was Jonathan Downes. He is the director of the Woolfardisworthy, England–based Centre for Fortean Zoology—one of the very few full-time groups in the world dedicated to the study of strange creatures such as the Chupacabra, the Loch Ness Monster, and the Abominable Snowman. Without a doubt, the most intense wave of activity occurred in the north of England in a town called Bolam—or, more specifically, at Bolam Lake, a large body of water that is itself a definitive hot spot for young lovers on Friday and Saturday nights.

It was on a freezing cold morning in January 2003 that Downes and his team of monster hunters drove up to Bolam from Downes's home in Devon—a mammoth convoy-style drive, to be sure. High strangeness hit the team—and in sinister fashion—just about as soon as they arrived. To his consternation, Downes found that all of his electrical devices—his computer, his cell phone, his audio equipment, and his cameras—were completely and utterly drained of power. All of them had to be charged before they could be used. This further bolsters the idea that "energy-eating" entities—in the form of Bigfoot—were wildly on the loose and had already had an effect on not just Jon Downes and his crew, but his devices too.

Of the many varied accounts given to Downes during his time at Bolam Lake, one of the most intriguing came from a man named Neil. In his 2004 autobiography, *Monster Hunter*, Downes says:

> Possibly the most astounding story that [Neil] had to recount had taken place a couple of summers before our visit. He had been in the woods at the opposite side of the lake with his girlfriend. They had been making love, when his girlfriend told him that she could see what she thought was a man in a monkey suit watching their sexual adventures intently from behind a bush. Neil, unsurprisingly looked around the area but could find nothing.

Very notably, Downes himself caught sight of the creature on one particularly dark night, in the woods around Bolam. Incredibly, Downes says that the thing looked like a huge, black-colored ape—but that it appeared to be one-dimensional, just like a shadow. This quite naturally brings up the issue of the Shadow People, which will be addressed later, with regard to how they have the disturbing ability to drain us of our vital energies.

While Downes is absolutely sure that the British Bigfoot phenomenon is all too real, he is of the opinion that the idea of colonies of giant apes roaming the UK is absurd—which it is. After all, there is no fossil record of apes ever having lived in the UK at all. Plus, there is the fact that the UK is very small, but has a population of more than sixty million. In other words, there is nowhere for such immense things to hide and not be caught by now. Downes concludes, therefore, that the Bigfoot of Britain is something supernatural in nature. We should listen to his opinions; he is a man who knows of what he speaks.

Goat-Man and the Farmer City Monster

A heading like this one sounds as if it should be the title of one of those awful movies that the Syfy channel insists on forcing upon us, such as *Chupacabra vs. the Alamo* and *Dinocroc vs. Supergator*. The following accounts, however, are all too real.

It was back in the summer of 1969 that sightings of a strange creature began to surface from the city of Lake Worth,

Texas, which takes its name from a large local lake. Although many of the reports suggest that the creature may have been a nomadic Bigfoot, it soon became known to one and all as the Goat-Man, based on the fact that some eyewitnesses claimed it had goat-like horns protruding from its hair-covered head. Hardly the kind of thing that you see every day!

Most of the stories had one thing in common: for the most part they came from couples parked in their cars late at night, deep in the woods of the lake, doing what couples have done ever since the car was invented. One such couple was John Reichart and his wife. Along with a couple of friends who were also there to have some fun, they found themselves confronted by the weird beast, and at the stroke of midnight, no less. It leapt onto the car's hood and left deep scratch marks along the side of the vehicle. The beast then quickly bounded off into the darkness. The fun was definitely over, and all four, filled with panic, quickly headed to the local police station. The story was taken very seriously by the local cops, who had no doubt that the four were in states of deep fear.

It wasn't long before the story reached the local media; the first story on the creature was titled "Fishy Man-Goat Terrifies Couples Parked at Lake Worth." It appeared in the pages of the Fort Worth-based *Star Telegram* on July 10, 1969. The article was written by none other than the late conspiracy theorist Jim Marrs, who passed away in 2017. It's intriguing to note that one of the witnesses to the

Goat-Man—a man named Jack Harris, a resident of Fort Worth—attempted to take a picture of the creature, only to find that his camera suddenly died on him. This is nearly identical to the situation Jon Downes found himself in at Bolam Lake in January 2003—decades later and on the other side of the world. The mystery of the Goat-Man soon came to an inexplicably sudden end. However, it's worth noting that reports still continue to surface every now and again, suggesting that the monster is far from being done with the people of Lake Worth.

One final thing on the Lake Worth Goat-Man: for many of the witnesses, the closest thing they could liken the creature to was a satyr of ancient Greek mythology. Satyrs had powerful sex drives. This connection was made by Dr. Karl Shuker, a cryptozoologist studying the encounters.

In light of this notable revelation from Dr. Shuker, perhaps the ancient people of Greece knew of the need that Goat-Man-type creatures had for sex—or sexual energy. Perhaps its voracious sexual appetite is what keeps the Goat-Man alive. The myths of the ancient Greeks may not just have been myths, after all. They may well have been based on personal knowledge of energy-based entities that plagued the people of Greece and fed on their sexual orgone thousands of years ago. Perhaps the satyr of ancient Greece and the Goat-Man of Lake Worth, Texas, were one and the very same.

Now it's time to take a look at the saga of the Farmer City Monster. We have legendary cryptozoologist Loren

Coleman to thank for digging deep into this situation, which lasted from May to August of 1970, in and around Marion County, Illinois. The Bigfoot-like animal was seen on more than a few occasions, including once by police officer Robert Hayslip, from Farmer City himself. It was in the early hours of the morning that Officer Hayslip saw the monster, which had piercing red eyes. Notably, the location was the area's very own local Lovers' Lane hangout.

Interestingly, Coleman found evidence of a very similar affair that went down in September 1965. The location was, yet again, one where young lovers regularly headed on weekend nights: Montezuma Hills, near Stevens Creek and just outside of Decatur. In this case, said Coleman, in his 2003 book, *Bigfoot!*, the foul-smelling and "massive, black, manlike shape" approached a car in which two couples were having a good time—until, that is, they were rudely interrupted. They didn't hang around. In other words, they got the hell out of Dodge, although the two boys did return later and claimed to have briefly seen the beast again.

Beware the Mothman

Between late 1966 and December of 1967, the people of Point Pleasant, West Virginia, found themselves in the icy grip of a fear-inducing monster. It became infamously known as the Mothman. Its name was most apt: the creature was described as being humanoid in form, but with a large pair of dark wings and eyes that blazed menacingly.

Numerous encounters with the beast were reported, all of them creating overwhelming terror in those who crossed its path. People saw the man-beast soaring in the sky late at night, lit up by a powerful moon. It chased terrified drivers on the dark roads around town—and matters all culminated in the collapse of Point Pleasant's Silver Bridge in December 1967. Dozens of those on the bridge at the time lost their lives, their vehicles plummeting into the churning waters below. Today, there are two prevailing theories within the cryptozoological community: that the Mothman caused the disaster; or that in its own strange way, it tried to warn people when the tragedy was looming. The jury is still very much out on that one.

It's most interesting to note that the bulk of the initial sightings of the monster occurred at—yes, you guessed it—Point Pleasant's very own Lovers' Lane. It was a place that was locally known as "the TNT area." There was a very good reason for that, and it had nothing to do with explosive fun on the backseats of cars. Today, the area is called the McClintic Wildlife Management Area. During the Second World War there was a processing plant for the production of TNT about five miles outside of town—hence the nickname. As for the storage area of the TNT, it was a nearby place in the woods where a number of secure, igloo-like buildings were constructed to house the highly dangerous and volatile materials. It was a bustling area, an important military facility that helped the Allies overcome the German soldiers and followers of Adolf Hitler. Indeed, at the height of things, more than three thousand people were employed at the factory. But that was the 1940s. By the 1960s the area was very different.

Friday and Saturday nights were when the woods were filled with cars. Guys and girls playing music, drinking beer, and having a blast. That's until the Mothman put an end to all of that. In November 1966, one of the most spectacular encounters with the monster was reported by Roger and Linda Scarberry and Steve and Mary Mallette. It wasn't long after the four reached the old plant that they encountered an approximately seven-foot-tall monster glaring at them in the shadows. They wasted no time exiting the area; the accelerator was floored and it wasn't long at all before they breathlessly shared their story with Deputy Millard Halstead of the local sheriff's office. The media had a field day with the story—a story which arguably set the scene for the mayhem that was to follow, and which culminated with the collapse of the Silver Bridge.

Today, the area is even spookier. The old TNT plant is no more; it has been razed to the ground and the area is fenced off. As for the decades-old igloos, they stand empty and abandoned, covered in overgrown bushes, vines, and moss. Graffiti adorns most of the igloos—some with imagery of Mothman himself. The setting—particularly at night—is apocalyptic, to say the least. Indeed, the ruined, run-down area looks like the kind of locale one might expect to see in the likes of *The Walking Dead*. And decades later it still oozes a sense of hard-to-describe menace.

Misery on Lovers' Lane

Notably, at the very same time that the events in Point Pleasant, West Virginia, were afoot, very similar things were going down in Huntington, New York; specifically, in an area known to the locals as Mount Misery. Like Point Pleasant, the area is steeped in weirdness and an atmosphere of high-strangeness prevails. Strange creatures—such as "black panthers" and ghostly black dogs with eyes like burning coals—roam the heart of the woods. Ghostly children have been seen wandering the old lanes after the sun has set. Pale-skinned Men in Black have knocked on the doors of locals late at night, warning them not to discuss the supernatural activity that dominates the area. And for years Mount Misery—with its thick, dense canopies of trees—has been a beacon for lovers.

John Keel reported in his 1975 book, *The Mothman Prophecies*, that midway through May of 1967, a young couple—Richard and Jane—were driving to Richard's home after an evening of hanging out and making out, when he suddenly fell sick. He was overcome by weakness and nausea and briefly passed out at the wheel. Fortunately, because of the tight corners on the small, winding roads, Richard was barely driving at fifteen miles per hour, something which allowed Jane to quickly grab the wheel and bring the car to a halt. The next thing Jane remembered was seeing a bright flash, followed by a groggy sense of missing time and a feeling of memories of... well, something, being erased from her mind. For Jane, all of this led her to believe that the light had come from a UFO and that she and Richard had been taken on board the craft—a definitive case of what today we would call an alien abduction.

Bringing matters up to more modern times, in 2008 there was a spate of deeply disturbing attacks on cats on the Lovers' Lane in Dallas, situated right in the heart of the city. Cats were found dead, sometimes violently torn apart, but on other occasions killed as if they had been dissected. In several of the cases—which always occurred in the dead of night—there was evidence of ceremonial activities being done under the cover of darkness. Quite understandably, this gave rise to the theory that there was a group in the area that was attracted to the world of the paranormal, a group that had killed the poor cats as a form of sacrifice to their demonic deities. The local media and the police covered the story extensively—particularly when the attacks began to increase and spread to Dallas's Lakewood Heights, Wilshire Heights, and Midway Hollow. Was it only a coincidence that most of the attacks occurred on Lovers' Lanes, a name that has, for decades, been so inextricably attached to the world of the supernatural? Many would likely suggest not.

In finality—at least as far as this chapter is concerned—what can we say about this strange phenomenon of terrifying paranormal activity on Lovers' Lanes around the country? As we have seen, sex is something that provokes not just powerful feelings, but incredibly powerful energies too. We know that much from the groundbreaking work of Wilhelm Reich. We also now know that where and when couples are engaged in sex—whether in the woods, on lonely roads after dark, or at places like Mount Misery that have a long history of strange phenomena attached to them—monsters suddenly, and far too conveniently, appear out of nowhere. And they so often appear right at the height of the sexual act, or immediately before or after. This is clearly not a coincidence. It's almost as if they are on the other side of a veil—a supernatural doorway—just waiting for the right time to allow them entry to our world, which may be *exactly* the case.

From Bolam Lake, England, to Lake Worth, Texas, and from Point Pleasant, West Virginia, to Farmer City, Illinois, these creatures surface when they know that sexual energy—orgone—is around and ready to be reaped. This may also explain why, at the site of the Mount Misery encounter in May 1967, the witness named Richard suddenly felt so weak—he was down on energy because he was being bled dry. We can make the same analogy with the failure of Jack Harris's camera in 1969, when he tried to photograph the Lake Worth Goat-Man. And very much the same can be said about Jon Downes's electrical equipment—cameras, a computer and more—all drained of power. It's all about energy and food.

In light of all the above, we can make a very strong case that sexual energy is one of the most important of all energies for these creatures of the night that are so reliant upon us, the human race, for their supernatural sustenance.

3
BLACK-EYED CHILDREN

There can be no doubt that one of the creepiest phenomena to have surfaced in the last two decades is that of what have become infamously known as the Black-Eyed Children (BEC). It would be overly simplistic to suggest that they are merely the offspring of the Men in Black (MIB) and Women in Black (WIB) who will surface later in this book. Admittedly, though, there are deep similarities, which will soon become apparent. And like the MIB and the WIB, the BEC are definitive drainers of energy. Before we get to this aspect of the story, let's first take a look at how, and under what specific circumstances, the Black-Eyed Children came to prominence. We'll also take a look at a few classic cases, none of which are particularly heartwarming (as if you really needed to be told that).

Although today there are people who claim to have seen the BEC in the period from the 1930s to the present day, the very first reported case didn't surface until January 1998. The location was the Lone Star State, specifically the city of Abilene. The story revolves around a man named Brian Bethel, a journalist who works for the *Abilene Reporter News*. It was late one night when Bethel's life was changed and he came to realize that there are dangerous, supernatural entities in our midst.

"Let Us In!"

It was close to 10:00 p.m. when Bethel had the kind of close encounter that one never, ever forgets. He pulled up at a mall not too far from his home to deposit a check in a mailbox. All was quiet and dark. Bethel, using the lights of the mall to illuminate the interior of his vehicle, was writing the check when he was rudely interrupted. He jumped with surprise at the sight of a couple of kids who were standing next to the car on the driver's side. But, there was something about these kids that rang alarm bells in Bethel's head. In fact, as Bethel would imminently learn, things were wrong in the extreme.

Bethel stared at the pair and couldn't fail to see just how incredibly pale the face of one of the boys was. The other had what Bethel described as olive-colored skin. Both boys were around ten to fourteen years of age, Bethel estimated, and both were dressed in pullovers. Only one of the two boys spoke—he claimed that they wanted to see a movie, *Mortal Kombat*, at the local cinema. But there was a problem: they had left their money at home. Could Bethel take them to their homes to get some cash? Bethel instantly realized that this whole situation had an air of dark and disturbing theater about it. There was an undeniably unsettling agenda at work, and it had absolutely nothing to do with movies.

Bethel awkwardly hemmed and hawed for a few moments, something that caused the talkative boy to become ever more insistent that Bethel let them in the car. Then things became downright eerie and chilling: Bethel found himself almost mind-manipulated, to the point that, to his horror, he could see that his hand was heading to the driver's-side door—*with the intent of opening it, but without his control.* Bethel, fortunately, broke the enchanting spell and didn't open the door after all. This clearly incensed the talkative boy, who amped up the pleas to allow them into Bethel's car. It was then, for the first time, that Bethel finally got a good look at their eyes. In his own words—in Pararational's May 16, 2013, post titled "Brian Bethel—The Black Eyed Kids"—Bethel stated, "They were coal black. No pupil. No iris."

The two boys realized that, by now, they were losing the battle to be permitted to get into Bethel's car. On this very point, Bethel himself said that the boy who did all of the talking "wore a mask of anger."

The boy, now displaying a look on his face that was part frustration and part anger, almost shouted: "We can't come in unless you tell us it's okay. Let us in!" Bethel, terrified, did nothing of the sort. What he *did* do was slam the car into reverse and head for home, completely panicked by the whole thing. Oddly, as he drove away, Bethel looked back only to see that the boys were nowhere in sight. In what was clearly an impossibly quick time, they had vanished.

And thus, a legend was quickly born. It's a legend that shows no signs of stopping. It's only getting worse.

When the Black-Eyed Children Demand Food

The West Virginia city of Point Pleasant is inextricably linked to the legend of the red-eyed Mothman, the flying fiend that terrorized the people of Point Pleasant from late 1966 to December 1967. In 2012, though, it was *black* eyes—rather than *red* eyes—which caused so much terror for one woman whom we'll call Marie. Although Marie's BEC experience occurred in 2012, she did not speak about it until two years later. She was in her mid twenties when she had an encounter she was destined to never, ever forget. Marie was still frightened when she related the facts to me at the 2014 Mothman Festival, which is held in Point Pleasant every September and attracts thousands of people.

Marie worked irregular hours at her job. As a result, one Saturday night shortly after 11:00 p.m., she was stretched out on her couch in front of the TV after a ten-hour stint at work. She had gotten herself a pizza and a couple cans of Coors Light. All was good. For a while.

Marie practically flew off the couch with fear as there was a loud knock on the front door of her second floor apartment. She thought, "Who the hell could that be at this time of night?" It was a very good question. Marie carefully and silently crept to the door and looked through the spyhole, her breathing already slightly labored. There were two boys staring back at her, both wearing black hoodies. She asked if they were okay. No reply. That wasn't a good sign. Marie put the chain on the door and then opened it the couple of inches that the chain would allow. One thing immediately struck Marie and filled her with fear: their skin was as white as a sheet of paper.

One of them, in a monotone and blank fashion, demanded food.

Not surprisingly, Marie slammed the door and ran to the furthest wall in the living room. Her mind was in a whirlwind of confusion and fear. After a few minutes, she again crept to the door and looked through the spyhole; the boys were still there. Most disturbing of all, the pair clearly reacted when Marie looked at them—even though she had done so in complete silence. Then, something even more terrifying happened: the pair of "children" suddenly shimmered—like a "heatwave," said Marie—and transformed into a pair of bipedal, lizard-like monsters. In seconds they were swallowed up by a sudden, black nothingness outside the door and were gone. It's hardly surprising that when she was satisfied that all was okay, Marie fled her apartment and went to stay with her mother in nearby Ohio for the next three days. Notably, for those three days Marie felt "exhausted," as if she had the flu. A coincidence? No.

A Creepy Boy and a Sinister Girl

Marie's reference to her pair of monstrous BEC demanding "food" is intriguing. As we have seen, her late-night visitors were clearly not flesh and blood entities—at least not in the way we see things. This strongly suggests that the kind of food they had in mind was something along the lines of prana energy. Certainly she felt depleted after the encounter. There are other BEC cases that add weight to this particular theory. We'll begin with the account of Martin, who lives just outside of Tecumseh, Oklahoma. Martin's encounter with the BEC went down in March 2011, and I was able to personally interview him just a few weeks after his experience. Like Marie, Martin was at home alone when he had just about the worst encounter possible.

As a brief aside, the fact that Martin, Marie, and Brian Bethel were *all* alone when they had their experience suggests a certain modus operandi at work. Namely, one that is designed to target people who are at their most vulnerable, when there is no one else around to help them. Even a cursory study of BEC history demonstrates that most witnesses are on their own when the Black-Eyed Children turn up. How the BEC know when and where to target people who are all alone is anyone's guess.

In terms of Martin's encounter, it occurred two days after he returned home. As a truck driver, he had been on the road for two weeks and was looking forward to a few days of relaxation and fun. He got neither. On his first night back, Martin planned on watching a bunch of shows he had recorded while he was away on the road. The evening began in completely normal fashion: he made himself a big sandwich, cracked open a cold beer, and watched his shows. Normality was about to go out the window. Around 8:30 p.m. there was that knock on the door, the kind that so many witnesses to the BEC have now experienced but surely wished they hadn't. Martin didn't even bother looking through the spyhole. He assumed it was his immediate neighbor, Rex, who would take in any packages from UPS and FedEx that might have been left on Martin's doorstep while he was away. Unfortunately for Martin, as he opened the door he instantly realized it was not Rex.

Hand in Hand and Mind to Mind

Martin got the shock of his life when he was confronted by a boy and a girl, both around eleven or twelve years of age, with large, black, eerie-looking eyes. The girl was dressed in jeans and a long-sleeve black top, while the boy had the almost-ubiquitous black hoodie. Both looked sickly and scrawny and as if they needed a hearty meal in them. Little did Martin know that this was *exactly* what they were there for. Hardly a fan of the supernatural, Martin had never heard of the BEC phenomenon and could only stand and stare at their curious faces, assuming at first that this was some kind of joke. But the Black-Eyed Children were certainly not laughing. They stood together, hand in hand, looking at Martin with expressions on their faces that were, paradoxically, lacking in emotion while giving off an air of highly charged malevolence.

Echoing Brian Bethel's encounter back in the 1990s, Martin said that when the girl said they were homeless and needed something to eat, it all seemed very much like a ruse—as if they had spoken the words time and time again. It was like a carefully crafted scheme on their part. Most disturbing of all, for a few moments Martin felt transfixed—almost hypnotized—by those large, black eyes. Indeed, he told me that he could not understand why he did not quickly shut the door at the sight of those terrible eyes. Martin could only say that it was as if he was somehow being prevented from shutting the door on the pair. One might be justified in saying that Martin had been placed in a state of full-blown mind control.

The girl repeated, "We need to eat. May we come in?" Martin said that he recalls her words accurately, and he felt that the girl's use of the term "may we?" (instead of "can we?") sounded like "how people talked way back." There is one missing portion from Martin's story. He recalls inviting them in—"it felt like I said it in a dream"—but then there are a few blank moments in his mind. The next thing he remembers is seeing the pair standing in front of him, while he sat on his living room couch, not knowing how he'd gotten there. The girl said just one word: *eat*.

At that point, Martin suddenly felt deathly ill. It was, he said, as if he "hadn't eaten in days." He explained that it was as if he himself was suddenly starving, but it was the children who needed to eat. The pair stared intently at Martin, who found himself getting weaker and weaker and weaker still. "Crashing" might be a more ideal term to use: Martin found himself barely able to move. Not because he was being prevented from moving, but because, physically speaking, he simply did not have the energy to even stand up. It was, Martin said, as if he himself was being eaten alive by the paranormal pair of ghoulish things in his midst.

After a few minutes, both the girl and the boy turned and left, still holding hands. Martin finally managed to crawl to his bedroom, where he lapsed into a deep sleep. He did not wake until well into the following afternoon. For the next three or four days, the overwhelming weakness—made worse by bouts of dizziness and a bad taste in his mouth—kept him in his bed. It was almost a week later when he finally felt fully back to normal. While Martin has no idea what the BEC were or are, he believes they were not human and somehow drained him of his energy.

An Early Encounter with a Black-Eyed Child

One final case will suffice when it comes to demonstrating how the Black-Eyed Children clearly see us as a food source. The story was given to me by the great-granddaughter of the witness, a woman whom I have dubbed Jane. Her experience is an interesting one, as it demonstrates that the BEC phenomenon is not the relatively new one that most people assume it to be. Jane, unfortunately, is no longer with us: she died in 1992 at the age of eighty-seven. Jane's great-granddaughter contacted me in 2016 to share the details of the encounter—which all of the family had heard of. It was kind of like the definitive skeleton in the closet: everyone knew of it, but no one really wanted to talk about it. At least, that is, until Jane's great-granddaughter related the facts to me.

At the time of her encounter, Jane was just eighteen years old. This would have put her encounter in 1923—which is astonishing, given that the BEC phenomenon is assumed to be one from fairly modern times. Jane and her family were living in a small town in eastern Louisiana. Times were hard and the family of seven struggled to make ends meet. If that were not enough, it was in January of 1923 that Jane had her first encounter with what can only be described as one of the Black-Eyed Children.

It was in the early hours of one particular morning that Jane awoke—unable to move and unable to speak—as a young boy dressed in black stood in her room, stretched out his hand, and pointed at her. Instantly, she began to feel ill and listless—the paralysis and inability to scream made things worse still. Then suddenly it was all over. The paralysis was gone, and so was the boy in black. Jane, practically hysterical, woke her parents and told them what had happened. The most terrifying part of the encounter? The boy's black eyes.

For the next three nights, the boy returned. The story was the same every night: the boy with the black eyes would manifest next to Jane as she lay in bed, unable to move an inch. As per the first time, he would reach out—the result of which was again a sudden feeling of overwhelming weakness. Although the boy never returned again, it took Jane—like Martin, decades later—days to get back to her normal self. Notably, in the immediate aftermath of the encounter, Jane had a series of nosebleeds—something that often occurs in paranormal situations. And she took on a slightly jaundiced appearance, which was most definitely not a good sign.

The story would undoubtedly never have surfaced had it not been for the fact that on one occasion in 2014, Jane's great-granddaughter was channel flipping and was confronted by a TV show that was focused in part on the BEC. Amazed and more than a bit disturbed, she realized what it was that Jane had encountered all those decades earlier: an energy-sucking thing that saw Jane as a convenient source of nutrition.

So, with all of that said, what exactly might the Black-Eyed Children be? The undeniable expert in this field is David Weatherly, a Texas-based author and paranormal investigator who has investigated dozens and dozens of

BEC-themed experiences. Notably, Weatherly suggests that the Black-Eyed Children may actually be the djinn—Middle Eastern entities that also feed on human energy. On this issue, Weatherly says the following in his 2011 book, *The Black Eyed Children*:

> As master shapeshifters, it would be no problem for the djinn to take the guise of a black eyed kid. Likewise, the chaos created in the lives of those who meet the children matches the pattern of the djinn's desire to create trouble for humans.

He adds, with an air of warning: "If the djinn are by chance behind the rash of black-eyed children encounters, the problem of the BEKs may be much more significant than it first appeared."

We should also give a significant amount of thought to the idea that the Black-Eyed Children are the unholy offspring of ancient Lilith.

Whichever scenario is the correct one, should you too—late one night—hear a banging on your front door and the cries of young children asking for food, whatever you do, keep that door locked. The food they are looking for just might be... *you*.

4
SHADOW PEOPLE

In the last decade or thereabouts, a great deal of research has gone into the phenomenon known as the Shadow People. Their title is most apt, as they appear in the form of a one-dimensional, flat shadow—usually in people's bedrooms while they sleep. Many of these entities—but certainly not all of them—have one thing in common: they wear an old-style fedora hat and a black suit. In that sense, there are similarities between the Shadow People and the Men in Black of UFO lore. It's fair to say that, for the most part, that's where the similarities end, apart from one important, extra thing: like the MIB they are intent on terrorizing those whom they maliciously target. And they do an extremely good job of it, too—unfortunately for us.

Precisely who or what the Shadow People are is a matter of deep debate. Jason Offutt is an expert on the subject, and the author of a 2009 book titled *Darkness Walks: The Shadow People Among Us*. He says there are eight different kinds of Shadow People—at least the ones we know about. He labels them as benign shadows, shadows of terror, red-eyed shadows, noisy shadows, angry hooded shadows, shadows that attack, shadow cats, and the Hat Man. Certainly, the last category—the Hat Man—is the one which is most often reported from all across the planet. Imagine a silhouetted character that stepped out of a 1940s/1950s-era piece of black-and-white film noir and you'll have a good idea of what the Hat Man looks like. That he is entirely shadow-like in nature only adds to the menace.

Heidi Hollis is an expert on this topic too, having penned a 2014 book on the subject, titled *The Hat Man: The True Story of Evil Encounters*. She has collected literally hundreds of reports of encounters with this particularly dangerous shadow-thing. One example from Hollis's files, which appears in her book, reads as follows: "Dear Heidi, I was maybe 5 years old when The Hat Man started to visit me. Every night I would lay in the top bed of my bunk bed and watch as my door would crack open for him to creep inside. As high up as I was, I would still have to look up to see him and I would freeze in horror at the sight of him!"

According to the witness, the Hat Man would lunge toward her at a phenomenal speed, and would always say, "One day I will have you!" To be sure, this was a deeply traumatic series of encounters for a young girl—a girl who never forgot the torment and the terror. At first glance, it may seem that the sole activity of the Shadow People is to create terror—and just for the warped sake of it. And yes, that is at least a significant *part* of the story. There is, however, another agenda to all of this. It's an agenda which has at its heart the goal of bleeding the witness dry of their life force.

A Shadow Person Causes Havoc in England

Considering that I have written three books on the Men in Black mystery and one on the interconnected issue of the Women in Black, I get a lot of feedback from readers about these creatures. Plus, the fact that many of the Shadow People are undeniably similar to MIB in nature and appearance— the black suit and the black hat being the most obvious parallels—ensures that I get a lot of reports that fall into this realm of darker-than-dark shadows. I'll share with you several such cases—all of which make a strong argument for the idea that the primary interaction between us and the Shadow People is feeding. And we're the banquet.

Margaret is a retired schoolteacher who lives in a small town in Wales. She had a series of encounters with a Hat Man–type Shadow Person back in 1967, which is long before most people had any inkling that such a phenomenon even existed. Admittedly, Margaret hadn't heard of it at the time— it was only in the 2000s, when the phenomenon grew and grew (and soon became a staple of the internet) that Margaret realized that what people were talking about was the shadowy creep who invaded her space way back in the sixties.

In 1967 Margaret was twenty-five years old and working and living in the English city of Bristol. All was looking good for Margaret: she had moved from her home city of Norwich, England, to Bristol to take on a new job teaching five-to-eight-year-old children. The work was fun, the kids were well-behaved, and all was well. Except when night fell. Margaret was hardly rich, so she rented a small room in a nineteenth-century, three-story house on the fringes of the city.

Only two nights after moving into the building, Margaret inexplicably woke up in the early hours of the morning. This was not typical for Margaret, who rarely ever had sleep issues. She put it down to nothing stranger than the move to a new environment and the new job. Nevertheless, she was at a loss to explain why she woke up in a state of overwhelming terror: her heart was racing and the bed sheets were soaked with sweat. After an hour or so, she managed to get back to sleep. Even more disturbing, though, upon waking up when her alarm clock rang, Margaret developed a sudden feeling that "there had been someone in the room." She didn't have any kind of conscious recollection of a particular, identifiable intruder, though. It was just an uneasy, hard-to-define feeling. That all changed on the next night.

It was hardly surprising that when Margaret went to bed the following night, her sense of unease—which had pretty much gone away during the day when her mind was focused on looking after a classroom full of kids—returned in spades. She tried to put it out of her mind and went to sleep. Three or four hours later, though, Margaret was wide awake. To her terror and horror, she found herself pinned to the bed by a shadowy figure—and I do mean that literally. It held her by the wrists and wore a large, black, brimmed hat. The unearthly thing straddled Margaret and moved its face toward her. She said, "I couldn't see anything at all; the face was just dark."

Things got worse: Although the monster appeared in shadow form, it bent even closer to her and kissed her on the lips. Margaret tried to scream as the thing put its black lips to hers and, in Margaret's own words, "began to take my life away; as if it was pulling the life out [of] me." Then suddenly the shadow was gone. Over the course of the next few months, the very same thing happened on four subsequent occasions. The weirdest part, however, was that on one occasion, as the shadow prepared to exit the room, it morphed into the form of a large black cat, then leapt off the bed and vanished into the darkness of the room.

This is particularly interesting, as there is a longstanding tradition of cats stealing the breath of babies. The tales of cats stealing the breath of newborns have a long history—in 1233 Pope Gregory IX maintained that cats were in league with the devil and had as many killed as was conceivably possible. The unforeseen result of this was the development of the legend of breath-stealing demonic kitties.

Thankfully, Margaret was never again assaulted by the Hat Man. By the way, she and her husband of forty-three years, Joe, share their property in Wales with a parakeet and a semi-tame fox that lives in the woods at the back of their home. But not a single cat. No surprise.

A Terrible Touch

Dan of Barstow, in San Bernardino County, California, had a very disturbing encounter with two Shadow People in early 2011. And just like Margaret's experience more than forty years earlier and a world away, the initial encounter prompted several follow-ups. A no-nonsense, tough biker, Dan is hardly the kind of person who is easy to intimidate and scare. But the shadow-things that intruded on his sleep—as he lay in a tent on the slopes of Mt. Rainier in Washington State in the summer of 2011—had Dan in a state of near hysteria. An enthusiastic outdoorsman, Dan spent four days hiking around the huge, fourteen-thousand-foot mountain, completely alone. He would live to regret doing that. It was around 3:00 a.m. one night when Dan woke with a start—and with an unsettling and intense feeling of being watched very closely. He lay still, holding his breath and clenching his fists. Something was definitely afoot—of that much he was sure. That's an understatement. In seconds, Dan was "rushed" by two skinny, spindly, shadowy monsters that were humanoid in appearance.

Dan suddenly found himself unable to move as the two figures hovered over him—at which point Dan said he felt incredibly weak, short of breath, and dizzy. A cold sweat enveloped him. All the while, the Shadow People had their index fingers on his stomach. It was only when they removed their silhouette-like fingers that the weakness went away, and normality suddenly returned as the pair exited the tent at a high speed. Dan didn't even try to get back to sleep; he leapt out of the tent, got all of his belongings together, jumped in his truck, and hit the road. It's intriguing to note that this issue of the Shadow People touching Dan's stomach is very reminiscent of the actions of the Black-Eyed Child that drained energy from Jane in Louisiana, back in 1923—by pointing at her. Unfortunately for Dan, this was not the end of things; the Shadow People were not about to leave Dan alone.

Three nights later, Dan had an almost identical experience—even down to the Shadow People once again touching his stomach with their fingers and causing him to feel suddenly weak and almost completely incapacitated. This time, though, the location was the living room of his Barstow apartment. The creatures came back on two more occasions: once several weeks later and the final time in August 2014—more than three years after the encounters had begun.

Dan had a deep suspicion that the Shadow People had the ability to take away his strength, to the point where he was so weak he could barely move. It was a sign that he had been "zapped"—to use Dan's very own concise description—by something that was feeding on him. Indeed, Dan was unable to shake off the idea that what he had encountered were akin to supernatural vampires, surfacing in the dead of night and on the prowl for a tasty feast—which they found in Dan himself. What particularly worried Dan, though, was that the Shadow People clearly knew where Dan lived. He remains baffled and concerned by this admittedly odd and unsettling issue.

5
HUNGRY GHOSTS

Imagine waking up with a start in the early hours of the morning and being confronted by one of the most terrifying-looking creatures that you could possibly imagine: a pale-skinned, humanoid monster with withered arms and legs, a huge stomach, an oversized neck, and a mouth smaller than a dime. It stares at you in malevolent style as it leans in close. You suddenly develop a terrible feeling that the monster is seeking out your life force, your vital energies, and your very essence. A sudden weakness and helplessness overwhelms you, as you seek to fight off the terrible thing that has suddenly invaded your space. In seconds it's gone, sated and satisfied by the fact that it has just fed on you. Whether you realize it or not, what you have just encountered is an ancient supernatural entity known as a *hungry ghost*.

The concept of the hungry ghost is not that well known in the West. That's because the phenomenon is very much one that has its origins in India and the Far East. It's tied to such issues as karma, how we choose to live on this physical plane, the consequences in the afterlife of having chosen the wrong path, and the form we may return in when we finally exit the physical plane.

The hungry ghost phenomenon is one that plays significant roles in the teachings of Sikhism, which came into existence in India in the latter years of the 1400s. The Sikhs—of which there are close to thirty million today—have their own sacred text, the Guru Granth Sahib. It teaches Sikhs to avoid what are known as the "Five Thieves." They are character traits which are seen as wholly unacceptable within Sikhism. Those traits are anger, greed, lust, ego, and attachment. Should a person go against the traditional teachings, Sikhs believe there is a very strong likelihood that the same person, after death, will return to our plane of existence in the form of a hungry ghost. Buddhists are deeply familiar with the hungry ghost phenomenon, too. Like Sikhism, Buddhism also originated in India—around the fifth century CE. Jainism, which is also an India-originated religion, maintains that reincarnation is a reality and that the hungry ghost phenomenon is inextricably tied to it—as we shall soon see. China's Taoism also has a tradition of belief in these malevolent spirits, as do the followers of Hinduism.

In other words, the hungry ghost concept is one known to various nations and cultures—and for a very long time, too.

Karma and Hungry Ghosts

While all of the above religions have significant differences—in terms of beliefs, the nature of the afterlife, and the specific definition of a supernatural creator—they are all pretty much in sync when it comes to one particularly relevant issue—namely, the idea that how one lives on earth will dictate how one will exist in the afterlife, the world to come. If you strive to live a good, honest life, the domain of the dead will embrace you in a positive fashion. If, however, you choose to live a lawless, evil, and hate-filled life, the outcome for you after you move on from the physical plane will be very different. In a worst-case scenario, you just might be cast back to the earth in the form of a hungry ghost.

It is the destiny of the hungry ghost to have an afterlife filled with torment, frustration, and rage. And a need to feed on the living, too. It's seldom that hungry ghosts are seen—chiefly, they only appear when they voraciously crave food. For the most part and for the rest of the time, they prefer to hide themselves away in the likes of caves, cellars, and old, dark abodes—in fact, just about anywhere that is free from the light of day. As for what, exactly, the hungry ghost needs and desires from us, it is all very much dependent on the aforementioned issue of karma. But what is karma? Let's take a look.

In a 2012 article, "The Meaning of Karma and How You Can Break Its Grip," Sadhguru—an Indian poet, author, and mystic—says, "Karma literally means action. We are referring to past action. From the moment you were born till this moment, the kind of family, the kind of home, the kind of friends, the things that you did and did not do, all these things are influencing you. Every thought, emotion and action comes only from past impressions that you have had within you. They decide who you are right now. The very way you think, feel and understand life is just the way you have assimilated inputs. We call this karma."

Karma is, arguably, just about the worst nightmare of the hungry ghost. If, in your physical existence, you were driven solely by greed—whether for money, riches, or power—you may find yourself returned as a hungry ghost whose greed revolves around food. Yet that infinitely tiny mouth—which is typical of the hungry ghost—prevents you from ingesting just about anything. Thus, you are in a state of never-ending frustration and a need to feed—which is why this particular form of spirit is called the hungry ghost. It is, quite literally, in a constant state of starvation that it tries to alleviate by targeting us.

Food for the Ghosts

In some cases, a hungry ghost will resort to one of the most sinister ways of feeding: it will target a person with a particularly vulnerable character. Weakness, insecurity, or a lack of self-esteem are all angles that the hungry ghosts will seek out and exploit. They will then possess the victim. The ghost's reasoning behind this is quite understandable. If the starving spirit is itself unable to eat, it will invade and take control of both the mind and the body of the person in its sights. In that sense, we're talking about something very similar to full-blown demonic possession, in which the mind of the victim is paranormally elbowed out of the picture and becomes the tool of the supernatural monster. The monster will quickly feed—greedily so—on just about anything and everything it can get its claws into when in the body of its human host. Then, when the creature exits the soul and mind of the person it briefly inhabited, it takes with it the energy derived from the food that was ingested by the possessed host. The hungry ghost is, then, one of the most manipulative of all the many and varied paranormal parasites that haunt our world.

It's not always quite so easy for the hungry ghost, though. The teachings of old state that some hungry ghosts will retain their ability to eat food and drink liquids, but that they will forever be thwarted from finding the nourishment they so deeply crave. For the hungry ghost who falls into this particular category, a cupboard will always be empty of food. A fridge will be bare. A stream will forever be dry. An oasis will be arid.

Then there are those hungry ghosts which are still able to find food after death, but whose mouths are so small that they cannot intake even the tiniest morsel. Karma will sometimes place a hungry ghost into a situation where there is an abundance of food, but as the creature closes in on the nourishing items they always catch fire, quite out of the blue. On other occasions, the food is corrupted—the suddenly rotten, stinking items cannot be eaten at all. It's all about teaching the hungry ghost a lesson for the way it lived in its physical life. It's a lesson that never ends.

A variation on all of this revolves around the hungry ghost of Japan. Its title is the Gaki. The Gaki, too, is cursed with an unending need to feed, but it can only digest human waste. A second Japanese hungry ghost is the Jikininki. It too is cursed. The only things it can ingest, physically at least, are the remains of the human dead. For that reason, Jikininkis are most often reportedly seen in graveyards and cemeteries, seeking out corpses both new and decaying—the Jikininkis don't care.

The fact that it is so difficult—and sometimes even completely impossible—for hungry ghosts to eat in the way we do explains why, for the most part, hungry ghosts will resort to inhabiting the minds of vulnerable people. It is through them that they can absorb the food-based energy. The hungry ghost does not stop there, though. Food as we understand it is not enough for them; they also secure a great deal of their vitality from what is known as Chi energy.

Chi Machine International states, in a 2017 article titled "CHI: Universal Life Force Energy," the following:

> Chi is the energy of life itself, recognized as the balance of Yin and Yang (male and female, positive and negative, electromagnetic energy), which flows through everything in creation ... When Chi becomes disturbed, stagnant, imbalanced or depleted, disease and illness begin to take form—the aura becomes darker and discolored, personal frequency vibrates incorrectly, and the meridians (energy pathways—Chinese origin), and chakras (energy centers—Indian origin), within the body, become blocked.

It is for this very reason—the intense syphoning of Chi energy by hungry ghosts—that so many people who have had the deep misfortune to encounter hungry ghosts find themselves constantly exhausted, generally unwell, and wide open to a whole variety of maladies. To say that people are being eaten alive and processed would not be far from the truth.

The Real Horrors Behind Halloween

As we have seen, the hungry ghost is predominantly an entity that has its origins in the religions and lore of India and Japan. It does, however, have a Western equivalent. This particular hungry ghost surfaces from its dark lair on what is without a doubt the spookiest night of the year. And what night might that be? Halloween, of course. For us in the twenty-first century, Halloween is just a bit of fun and excitement on October 31. Kids dress up as zombies, as ghosts, as ghouls, and as monsters. Costume parties are held. Pumpkins are bought in the millions. The words "trick or treat?" echo around much of the planet. And a good time is had by one and all. Few people, though, have an understanding of why we celebrate Halloween in the fashion we do. You may be surprised to learn that the festival has the hungry ghost phenomenon at its heart. Yes, really.

The name Halloween is taken from a term coined way back in the 1500s, that of All Hallows' Eve. It is also linked to what is called All Saints' Day, which is celebrated on November 1—just twenty-four hours after Halloween begins. Both Halloween and All Hallows' Eve have much older origins that can be found in ancient Gaelic and Pagan rites and rituals. They extend back to at least the tenth century. Collectively, those rites and rituals were known as Samhain. It was on the night of the Samhain, the ancients believed, that the dead—or perhaps the *un*dead—would walk the planet. They would come knocking on the doors of the people who so deeply feared the very things that would manifest in our realm on the night of October 31.

While some of the spectral visitors were friendly, others most definitely were not. As a result, Samhain was all about trying to appease the dead, to honor them, and to respect them. And not to incur their terrible wrath. While Samhain lore states that the dead were unable to physically eat food, those same spooks were invited to sit in on the immense banquets that were prepared for October 31. If nothing else, the hope was that the spirits would see the invite as something positive and symbolic and that the dead would not rise up against the living. That is why today kids all over the world ask that same, universal question: "Trick or treat?" It basically means "Will you give me food or will you pay a terrible price?"

On the night of Samhain, if it was suspected that particularly hostile spirits were wandering the landscape, people would disguise themselves as the very monsters that they were so frightened of. In other words, it was an ingenious form of camouflage. This old tradition, too, has become inextricably incorporated into Halloween. It's precisely why kids are encouraged to dress as skeletons, zombies, and demons: whether they know it or not, they are continuing a ritual that dates back centuries, which is designed to appease and hide from the hungry ghosts that would surface on Samhain.

When Jack and the Devil Clashed

Even Halloween's famous jack-o'-lantern has its origins in paranormal food and the world of the supernatural. In Ireland, there is an ancient tradition of a legendary character called Stingy Jack, a man who spent most of his life as drunk as a skunk. On one occasion, Jack got the best of none other than the devil himself: he manipulated the overlord of hell to climb an apple tree and get him a tasty apple to eat. Not realizing that there was cunning deceit at work, the devil saw no problem in doing that. While the devil was climbing the tree, however, Jack carved the sign of the cross into the trunk of the tree—which prevented the devil from coming down. Jack then demanded that the devil agree to never take his soul. The horned and fork-tailed one was outraged. Unfortunately though, the devil had no choice: if Jack didn't obliterate the cross from the tree, the devil would be stuck up in the tree forever. Against all the odds, Jack had achieved something incredible: he had trumped the devil.

When, as an old man, Jack finally died, he was denied entry to heaven because of his drunken ways. And the devil wanted nothing to do with him either—he had not forgotten that long gone day when Jack had bested him. At the time that Jack was face to face with the ruler of hell, he was eating a turnip. Filled with rage, the devil hurled a hot coal at Jack—which Jack caught—just as he was about to return to our reality in the form of a ghost. Given that both heaven and hell were off-limits to Jack, he decided to walk the landscape by night, seeking—but never, ever finding—a final resting place on earth. And how did Jack negotiate the land by night, when the skies were dark? He placed the devil's glowing coal into the turnip and used it as a torch to illuminate his way. And that's why, today, we have the tradition of placing a candle or a light in a pumpkin. And, of course, on the matter of parasites, we should not forget that Jack is part and parcel of the "Trick or Treat?" phenomenon—the treat usually being a form of food.

Clearly, even though the concept of the hungry ghost originated in India and Japan, the Gaels and the Pagans knew enough of the hungry ghost phenomenon that it was seen as vitally important to provide the dead with food on October 31—even if it was just in the form of a symbol of friendship and kinship, rather than literal food. It's highly ironic that so few people have heard of the hungry ghost phenomenon, and the ability of those same spirits to drain us of much-needed energies. Yet on October 31 millions of people bask in the old days of Samhain, without realizing its origins in Paganism and the dead walking among us.

6
BLOODSUCKERS

There is one particular paranormal parasite that just about everyone has heard of, regardless of whether or not they have an interest in the subject. It's the vampire. For the most part, the image of the vampire has been dictated by popular culture, such as movies, television shows, and novels. The vampire of the past was typically presented in the form of a middle-aged man dressed in a black suit and cloak. Today, though, Hollywood's vampires are far more likely to resemble a cross between Rob Zombie and Marilyn Manson. Because the vampire is such an integral part of horror fiction, it has led to the assumption that bloodsucking monsters of the night don't exist outside of the imagination. This is, however, very much at variance with the facts. It's somewhat ironic that to understand why the vampire has taken on such an iconic stance we have to first look at the world of entertainment.

There is absolutely no doubt at all that the vampire—as we know it today, at least—would not exist without one particular book. That title is Bram Stoker's *Dracula*, which was published in 1897. As we'll now see, though, Stoker's classic gothic novel was certainly not the first work to tell a fear-filled saga of the bloodsucking undead. But it was definitely the most visible and popular.

The Dawning of the Vampire in Fiction

It should be noted that *Dracula* was a definitive Johnny-come-lately. For example, in 1819—almost eighty years before Stoker's book surfaced—John William Polidori penned *The Vampyre: A Tale*. For years, it was incorrectly attributed to George Gordon Byron, better known as Lord Byron, an acclaimed poet and politician. His most famous piece of work was the epic poem *Don Juan*. Polidori was Byron's physician and close friend, and also penned *The Fall of the Angels* and *On the Punishment of Death*.

The Vampyre: A Tale was published in 1819 in the pages of *The New Monthly Magazine*. The central character is a somewhat Dracula-like figure. He is one Lord Ruthven, a dangerous and deadly character—indeed, just about anyone and everyone who crosses his path is destined for tragedy. As Polidori's story reveals, Lord Ruthven is a definitive drainer and drinker of blood. A precursor to the famous saga of Count Dracula? Definitely. Such was the success of the story—and the fascination with Lord Ruthven—that other writers of the day continued where Polidori finished and wrote their own stories concerning the evil lord. They included Cyprien Bérard's 1820 novel, *Lord Ruthwen ou les Vampires*.

Then, in 1847 *Varney the Vampire; or, the Feast of Blood* caught the attention of the people of the UK when it appeared in a "penny dreadful" publication. Written by Thomas Peckett Prest and James Malcolm Rymer, the saga of vampiric Sir Francis Varney became a huge success, further cementing the image of blood-swilling monsters in then modern-day England. *Carmilla*, published in 1871–72 and written by Joseph Sheridan Le Fanu, is a highly atmospheric novella, which sees the female vampiric Carmilla of the title attracted to and obsessed with Laura—the protagonist of Sheridan Le Fanu's tale—which emphasizes the sexual and erotic aspects of vampirism.

But no one can deny that it was Bram Stoker's *Dracula* that really got the ball rolling, in terms of making the vampire known both far and wide. While *Dracula* is certainly seen as the number-one vampire-themed novel, it's unfortunate that those titles that came before it have largely been forgotten by most people—apart from firm devotees of the genre.

Without Bram Stoker's gothic masterpiece, there would not have been Universal's 1931 movie by the same name, which starred Bela Lugosi. Nor would there have been such sequels as *Dracula's Daughter* and *Son of Dracula*. And, had Universal's movies not have been such phenomenal successes, it's all but certain that Christopher Lee would not have been given the chance to make the role his own in numerous movies from Hammer Film Productions, including *Scars of Dracula*, *Taste the Blood of Dracula*, *The Satanic Rites of Dracula*, and *Dracula AD 1972*. Would we have had *'Salem's Lot*? *Interview with the Vampire*? *Twilight*? *True Blood*? *The Strain*? Almost certainly not.

The phenomenal and combined success of all the above movies, TV shows, and novels has exposed the vampire to millions of people over the course of a couple of centuries. These same productions have achieved something else, too: a widespread assumption that vampires are only fictional in nature—which, as incredible as it may sound, is far from the case. That's right. Those bloodsucking monsters that you were told didn't really exist... *really do*. And they have for millennia.

Vampires: the Real and Ancient Kind

The term "vampire" was not used in the English language until the 1700s, when it appeared in the pages of *Travels of Three English Gentlemen* in 1746. Nevertheless, tales of marauding, deadly blood-drainers—in human form—can be traced back to the dawning of history and civilization. Lilith—quite possibly the most dangerous bedroom invader of all—was said to not just have sex with men as a means to "steal" their sperm, but also to take their blood. Joseph McCabe noted that the Lilith-like Lilu and Lilitu of ancient Babylonia caused the victims of their attacks to fall sick with anemia—a sure and certain sign that blood was extracted from those same victims to a dangerous degree.

The people of India believed in the dreaded ghostly band of creatures called Vetala. Although they were spirit-based in nature, they also had the ability to drain the living of blood. They were also known for bleeding fresh corpses dry—they would lurk in the shadows of old cemeteries and graveyards, patiently waiting for darkness to blanket the landscape, at which point they would dig deep and fast into the ground, seeking out that most precious commodity of all: blood.

Empusa was very much a Lilith-type entity who tormented the people of Greece thousands of years ago. Just like Lilith, Empusa—a beautiful woman with a disturbing craving for blood—would creep up on the unwary in the dead of night and drain them of blood. Whereas blood and sperm were all that Lilith needed, Empusa would also devour the flesh of her victims. The early Greeks also feared Lamia, a female blood-drinker who was the secret lover of Zeus—the Greek god of thunder—and fed on the blood and flesh of children. The ghostly Gello of Greek lore also spent most of her time seeking out the young to extract their blood, specifically to make it hers.

A Blood-Drinking Fog Monster

Moving on to Scandinavia circa 1,100 years ago, we have tales of a violent and incredibly powerful monster of human-like proportions, known as the *draugr*. Its alternate title: the *aptrgangr*. Both roughly translate as "one who walks after death." It would be best described as a vampire with zombie-like overtones, since this particular vampire wasn't just partial to human blood; it also had a taste for human flesh. Scandinavian lore maintained that to ensure the dead never rose up and attacked the living, all human bodies should be buried in horizontal fashion. If a corpse was interred even slightly angled, there was a very good chance that it would return as a dangerous draugr. Even failing to pay the newly dead the respect they deserved might cause a man, woman, or child to come back as a draugr—and come back quickly, too.

These creatures were not just ferocious drainers of blood and eaters of flesh, though. They also had a fascination with gold, silver, and millennia-old treasures, which they would obsessively hoard. They also possessed supernatural abilities, including the power to turn themselves into a thick fog in that ethereal form—which prevented them from being killed. After all, it's impossible to plunge a wooden stake into fog. As a result, putting an end to a draugr was an arduous and highly dangerous task.

Returning from the Grave

Certainly, one of the most notorious of all the vampires was Jure Grando. He was a resident of Kringa, in what today is Croatia. The term "vampire" was still unused at the time, but the local folk had their very own title for the bloodsucking monsters of the area. They called them the "strigoi," which was also the term used in the popular show *The Strain*, which was broadcast on the FX channel from 2014 to 2017.

Grando lived all of his life in the area and passed away in his late seventies. He wasn't ready to give up on his life, however. He came back as a dangerous vampire with a wild craving for blood. Interestingly, whereas most vampires are said to return in undead form within days of their original passing, with Grando about a decade and a half passed before he reappeared on the scene. He quickly instilled fear in the people of Kringa.

To begin with, Grando caused absolute hysteria for many people by staring malevolently through the windows of the homes of the village folk and scaring them out of their wits—this included Grando's widow. Rumors flew around the area that whenever Grando knocked on someone's door, they would soon be snared by the Grim Reaper. The local priest, Father Giorgio, was finally able to confront the vampiric Grando with a cross—which clearly had an effect on the deadly thing, to the extent that he fled away at a phenomenally high speed.

The day after the confrontation between Father Giorgio and Grando proved to be the latter's final day—or final night, rather—on earth. Having learned that each and every morning before sunrise Grando returned to his grave, the locals chose to take care of things when he was at his most vulnerable: sleeping in his wooden box. The coffin was hauled out of the ground and carefully opened. All were shocked and horrified by the sight before them: there was Grando, sporting an evil-looking, maniacal grin, but fully asleep. Father Giorgio said prayers while one of the townsfolk, Stipan Milašić, sliced Grando's head clean off his shoulders. Grando awoke, screaming, as the blade cut into him, but it was too late: the vampire's life force was already ebbing away. Finally, the good folks of Kringa were safe from the terrible strigoi.

Terror in Mexico

Panteón de Belén is the name of a cemetery which can be found in Guadalajara, Mexico. Just like so many cemeteries all around the world, it has a deeply sinister vibe surrounding it—one that still persists today, almost 170 years after it was built. Most of the residents of the cemetery do what they are supposed to do: namely, stay at rest. One, however, did not. According to stories that surfaced during filming of a Syfy channel show, in the latter part of the nineteenth century, one particularly restless character roamed the cemetery, which led to horror and even death. Matters began when the blood-drained body of a woman was found late at night on nearby Nardo Street. Her body was discovered in an alleyway off the street, with nothing less than a savage wound to the neck—specifically, to the jugular vein.

Days later, yet another body was found, this time on the fringes of the cemetery itself. This one, however, had been dug up from the grave in which it had been buried just days earlier. The dangerous monster that was responsible had dug deep into the grave and wrenched the lid of the coffin off. Yet again, there was the classic calling card of a vampire: two bites to the neck. Over the following week, several children were killed—all in the very same fashion. Clearly, something had to be done, and quickly. It was.

Within forty-eight hours of that weeklong period of savagery, there was yet another death, this one of a young girl, whose body was found discarded in the cemetery. The violent mode of attack was as it has always been for a vampire. The fact that most of the attacks either occurred in the Panteón de Belén cemetery, or around it, led the townsfolk to conclude that the best approach was to keep a stealthy and watchful eye on the place. It worked: in the early hours of one morning, the creature was yet again prowling around the graves, seeking out fresh corpses, when a gang of men suddenly appeared out of the shadows and surrounded the snarling, staring abomination. It took more than a few men to force the beast to the ground. And as it violently fought and struggled to make its escape, one of the group hammered a wooden stake into its heart. The undead was now dead—period.

Determined to ensure that the vampire of Guadalajara would never again kill or cause mayhem, the people of the area quickly buried the remains of the fiend in a deep grave. Then, for good measure, they covered the body with layer upon layer of concrete—with the stake still in its heart. In situations like this, it's far better to be safe than sorry. The story is still not quite over, though. It was only around six or seven weeks later when the concrete slab started to fracture. It was not, however, due to the bloodsucking creature finding a way out. Rather, it was caused by a large nearby tree, the huge and thick roots of which were pushing against the concrete and making it look as if the vampire was the cause. This aspect of the saga has led to the development of a story that, in the area, still exists today.

Local lore tells of a tree in the cemetery that bleeds when its bark is cut into. What kind of blood? Human blood.

In all likelihood, this aspect of the story is a piece of folklore—but born out of an all too real story of vampirism, bloodsucking, and terror. We're finished, now, with the nightwalker of Guadalajara, but we're certainly not done with cemeteries. It's now time to take a trip to England. The time? The late 1960s.

On the Loose in London

In relatively modern times, there are few stories quite as strange and sinister as that which concerned a fearful monster called the Highgate Vampire, on account of the name of the old London cemetery where the creature lurked, slaughtered, and, of course, drank. It was in the 1960s that Highgate Cemetery found itself inhabited by a most unwelcome visitor: a seven- to eight-foot tall monster with bright red eyes, an evil-looking and gaunt face, and pale skin, who wore a flowing black cloak. Amid the old graves, a dangerous parasite roamed by night.

As for Highgate Cemetery, it was opened in 1839, is located in north London, and is composed of the East Cemetery and the West Cemetery. It's a huge and undeniably atmospheric place that extends close to forty acres in size. Catacombs abound, as do moss-covered, crooked gravestones. The dead are everywhere. The cemetery is also dominated by huge trees, endless bushes, and a massive variety of plants—not to mention a large fox population, owls, and birds of prey. In fact, so revered are Highgate Cemetery's wooded areas that it has officially been listed as a "Historic Park and Garden" by the British government.

It's not at all surprising that when the sun has set, when the land is shadowy, and when daylight is gone, the cemetery takes on an eerie air. The hoot of an owl, the creaking of the branches of an old tree, and the sight of many battered gravestones all combine to send chills up and down the spines of more than a few who know the legend of the resident vampire. And in decidedly synchronistic fashion, Hammer Film Productions' 1970s movie *Taste the Blood of Dracula* was partly filmed in Highgate Cemetery.

When Fact and Fiction Cross

Cemeteries are creepy places at the best of times. In the 1960s, however, the atmosphere at Highgate became distinctly chilled—maybe even freezing. Skulls and even partial human skeletons were found strewn around Highgate Cemetery, which at the time was very much overgrown—largely because the entire place had been left to fall into rack and ruin, something that only amplified the air of mystery and fear that dominated the area. It should be noted, though, that long before the events of the 1960s began, there was *already* a vampire tradition at Highgate Cemetery. The story has a connection to none other than the man who brought Count Dracula to life: Bram Stoker.

It's most intriguing to note that in *Dracula*, Stoker made mention of the old cemetery being the final resting place of one of the deadly count's followers. It's possible that Stoker was inspired by an all too real set of eerie circumstances that occurred in the 1800s. In 1855, a woman named Elizabeth Siddal was buried in the cemetery. She didn't stay there for too long, though: in 1862, her grave was opened up. The reason we're told is that the family wanted to recover a number of poems that Siddal had written that were interred with her. To the horror of everyone present, after seven years spent six feet under, Siddal looked exactly as she did in life: her corpse had not decayed and her red hair looked freshly washed and dried. The implication was that Siddal was one of the undead—a vampire.

On this point, in a 2013 blog post titled "Elizabeth Siddal—The First 'Vampire' of Highgate?," Redmond McWilliams wrote, "Some notable literary scholars have theorised that the fictional character of Lucy Westenra, one of Count Dracula's disciples, was largely based on Elizabeth Siddal: the late wife (and muse) of pre-Raphaelite painter Dante Gabriel Rossetti." It's almost certainly not a coincidence that Bram Stoker chose to feature the old cemetery in his classic novel.

Supernatural Sixties

In the 1960s, tales began to surface of a fiery-eyed vampire on the loose in London's Highgate Cemetery. There were stories of people going missing, of graves allegedly desecrated, and of bodies vanished under mysterious circumstances. The creature was also seen roaming around at night in the old Swains Lane area, its grim and cruel visage sending people into states of unbridled terror. One of the most significant cases took place in late 1969. The story was both strange and creepy: The witness in question was taking a walk through the cemetery when he suddenly became disoriented—which was strange, as he knew the area very well. He also felt weak and sick, which is something we have seen time and again in relation to numerous confrontations with paranormal parasites. Suddenly, a black-garbed, red-eyed terror loomed into view—hovering several feet off the ground. The man did his utmost to flee the area, but it was all in vain. The creature got closer as the man got progressively weaker—which, with hindsight, led the man to believe the monster was draining him of his life, of his vital energies.

The publicity surrounding the alarming incident prompted others to come forward who had also seen the vampire of Highgate Cemetery. One witness, while walking her dog through the thick and unkempt trees late one night, encountered a shrieking, banshee-like thing that sailed through the air, then suddenly dematerialized.

Another person who saw the monster at close quarters was David Farrant, a paranormal investigator who decided to check out the cemetery for himself. It was a case of "be very careful of what you wish for." With midnight less than an hour away, and on the monster-haunted Swains Lane, Farrant suddenly developed a sense of something deeply malevolent in his midst. He strained his eyes, staring intently into the darkness of the cemetery, and realized that there was something staring back at him. Was it merely a trick of the light? No, unfortunately it was not. Farrant had barely gotten fifteen feet into the cemetery when he saw, to his horror, a tall figure in black. Like several of the earlier witnesses to the vampire, Farrant felt his self-will leaving him—and rapidly, too. Luckily for Farrant, the entity suddenly vanished, leaving him frazzled and traumatized.

The Media, the Monster, and Latter-Day Reports

As a new decade dawned—the 1970s—Highgate Cemetery's resident vampire was still causing terror and mayhem. Numerous people contacted the local *Hampstead & Highgate Express* newspaper to share their encounters with the thing. One of those people—R. Docherty—whose story was published in the paper, stated, "There is without a doubt a ghost. Of when and whom he originated I do not know. Many tales are told, however, about a tall man in a hat who walks across Swains Lane and just disappears through a wall in the cemetery. Local superstition also has it that the bells in the old disused chapel toll whenever he walks." The above quote can also be found in Neil Arnold's 2010 book, *Paranormal London*. We'll hear more about Arnold shortly.

Realizing that tales of monsters and spooky places sell newspapers, the staff of the *Hampstead & Highgate Express* ran an article in 1970 titled "Does a wampyr walk in Highgate?"—*wampyr* being an old German term for a vampire. The interest in and intrigue surrounding Highgate Cemetery's resident monster was increasing rapidly. The newspaper quoted the words of Sean Manchester, of the British Occult Society. Manchester said that he believed the vampire originated in Turkey, and that its followers "eventually brought him to England in a coffin at the beginning of the eighteenth century and bought a house for him in the West End [of London]."

The ongoing publicity prompted a young woman to come forward with her own account of an encounter with the creature as she walked past the old cemetery late one night. The pale-faced thing threw her to the ground and vanished into the darkness. Things got even more bizarre when two young men, James White and Simon Wiles, were arrested by the police. The pair was seen prowling around the cemetery and brandishing nothing less than a wooden stake and a crucifix! The police took an extremely dim view of the attempts of the two to slaughter the vampire, but no charges were ever brought. Certainly, it's doubtful that killing a vampire could even be considered a crime.

By 1971, the sightings—and the accounts of people feeling "drained" by the monster—came to a mysterious halt. That is, until decades later—specifically, in 2006.

Neil Arnold is someone who has extensively investigated the many and varied paranormal mysteries of the UK's capital city. Notably, he has uncovered post-1970s sightings of the Highgate Vampire. In his 2010 book, *Paranormal London*, Arnold stated that on one particular night in the summer of 2006, "a man walking down Swains Lane saw a dark figure standing near the gates of the West Cemetery. Upon approaching, the man noticed that the figure was dressed in a long, dark coat and had a tall, black hat perched on its head."

The figure in black said "good evening, sir" to the somewhat disturbed man. That disturbed feeling was quickly replaced by sheer terror when the figure rose off the ground, floated across the road, and vanished into the shadows of the cemetery. Then, one year later, a glowing-eyed figure in black was also seen on Swains Lane and it walked through a solid brick wall. Perhaps one day the energy-draining vampire of Highgate Cemetery will return, once again causing terror and mayhem, just as it did back in the late 1960s and early 1970s.

Moca's Monstrous Vampire

When it comes to the issue of paranormal activity on the island of Puerto Rico, there's no doubt that the legendary Chupacabra leads the pack. Twenty years before the Chupacabra surfaced, however, there was another monster roaming the island. It became known as the Moca Vampire, on account of the municipality in which the creature lurked and hunted.

The mystery and controversy began in early 1975. Witnesses described seeing a large, winged monster swoop down on farm animals, killing them instantly and drinking their blood. Imagine something that was part pterodactyl, part giant bird, and part Mothman, and that will give you an idea of the nature of the beast, which fed on not only small animals like chickens and geese, but even on cows and pigs. It always emitted an earsplitting shriek as it dive-bombed the unfortunate animals and killed them with one swipe of its sharp claws. For two terrifying weeks, the Moca Vampire had the people of the area living in fear—and no one can blame them for that. Then, mysteriously, the monster was gone and the attacks were over. The creature was never seen again—unless, of course, you subscribe to the theory that the Chupacabra and the Moca Vampire are actually one and the same, but with different names, which is admittedly not impossible.

As we have seen, the vampire, which many people assume to be a fictional entity largely created by Bram Stoker and portrayed in masterful fashion by Bela Lugosi and Christopher Lee, is an all too real monster. It's a blood-draining, diabolical thing that has been with us for millennia and shows no signs of going away anytime soon. Remember that, should you ever decide to take a trip to Puerto Rico.

And remember to take a couple of stakes and crosses with you, too.

7
MIND MONSTERS

Now we come to one of the strangest of all the many and varied supernatural creatures that feed upon us. It goes by two names: the *tulpa* and the *thought-form*, although they are one and the same. The concept of the tulpa began centuries ago within the culture and beliefs of Tibetan Buddhists. In essence, a tulpa is a creature that is created and driven by the power of human imagination. If that sounds strange … well yes, it *is* strange!

Essentially, it goes like this: If you focus your attention on a particular image—let's say, for the sake of argument, that of a fiery-eyed, leathery-winged gargoyle—you can give it some semblance of reality, and eventually an independent existence. You lie down on your bed, late at night, when and where you won't be disturbed, and you focus intently on your legendary monster of choice. You carefully visualize its form, those huge wings, its malevolent face, and its clawed hands. Perhaps you even give it a long and powerful tail. You focus on the image of the beast flying high above the rooftops of your own town in the dead of night. And you repeat that process night after night, week after week, and maybe even month after month. You may even utilize meditative techniques to allow you to enter altered states of mind, which will serve to amplify the imagery even more.

Then one day, reports suddenly begin to surface in your town of what sounds just like the very beast that you have been so deeply focusing on in the depths of your mind and imagination. In essence, you have successfully created a monster—solely by thinking it into existence. No, the monster is not of the flesh and blood variety, but it lives and thrives all the same. And you—and you alone—are responsible for it. A wholly fictional entity is now active and living in our world.

Food for Thought

Given the theme of this book—how supernatural entities use us as their fuel—two important questions need answering: How, exactly, does the tulpa feed on us? And *why* is it so driven to feed on us?

A fully mature thought-form cannot exist without one particular thing: a strong and widespread belief in its existence. In other words, the tulpa does not feed on us physically. Instead, it dines on our beliefs.

As more and more people come to believe that the creature is real, it gains a greater and more intense foothold in our world, and becomes more and more corporeal in nature. If interest in and acceptance of the monster attains huge heights, another issue surfaces: eventually, the creature is no longer reliant on the beliefs of its creator to survive. In the early stages, a tulpa will certainly hover around its creator. As it grows stronger, though, the tulpa leaves its moorings behind and effectively draws in the beliefs of anyone and everyone that accepts it's real. The disturbing side of all this is that, in almost all situations, when the tulpa is fully energized—by the collective beliefs of not just hundreds of people, but thousands, or maybe even millions—it takes on a deeply malevolent streak. It rapidly becomes evil and dangerous.

On top of that, to ensure that the belief in the tulpa continues, the monsters of the mind need to be continually seen. After all, if people don't see them, they forget about them. And when that happens, the tulpas eventually crumble, fragment, and disintegrate into irreversible nothingness. In very much the same way that we cannot survive without food and water, the tulpa cannot survive without basking in that collective belief of untold numbers of people. In that sense, the tulpa doesn't just *want* us to believe in it, it *needs* its junkie-like fix of belief, and it needs it constantly.

Summoning a Spider God— and Living to Regret It

It's time, now, to take a look at the case of a man named Richard Freeman; it's a case that perfectly demonstrates how a tulpa can be created and how the outcome can be dark and harrowing for everyone involved. Formerly a head keeper at England's Twycross Zoo, Freeman has a deep interest in the field of cryptozoology, which is the study of unknown animals such as Bigfoot, the Loch Ness Monster, Mothman, the Chupacabra, and the Abominable Snowman. Freeman is convinced that many such cryptids are flesh and blood animals that the domains of science and zoology have yet to categorize and classify. He also believes, though, that at least *some* such creatures may well be tulpas. To try and prove the point, back in the 1990s Freeman set out to create his very own abominable monster.

As a goth and a dedicated fan of the writing of the likes of Clark Ashton Smith and H. P. Lovecraft, Freeman chose to make his particular tulpa of choice a huge, horrific spider of truly malevolent proportions. Freeman's inspiration for his creation was Smith's spider deity, Atlach-Nacha. It appears in Smith's story *The Seven Geases,* which was published in 1934. Atlach-Nacha is described as a terrifying, malevolent arachnid that has a somewhat human-looking, hairy face, and huge, spidery limbs. It lives in a dark, subterranean world filled with winding and near-endless caves that can be found far below the fictional Mount Voormithadreth. Interestingly, Smith's monster straddled two domains: that of the dream state and that of the real world, which is exactly what the tulpa does too. It's a construct of the mind that very seldom stays there. All of which brings us back to Richard Freeman.

It was the summer of 1997 and, at the time, Freeman was a student at the University of Leeds in England, where he was working toward a degree in zoology. When Freeman decided to try to create a tulpa version of Atlach-Nacha, he took the whole thing very seriously, certainly a vital key to ensuring a high degree of success. He enlisted the help of several friends at the university. One and all set about constructing what can only be described as an altar to the monstrous spider-thing in the cellar of the house where they were all living. As well as constructing the altar, Freeman and his friends took a large piece of cloth, painted it to look like a vast spider's web, and hung it up in the cellar. Then, at the foot of the altar, they began a complex series of rites and prayers, all designed with one goal in mind: to bring Clark Ashton Smith's monster to life—a sort of life, at least. The group collectively concentrated on the image of the hideous spider deity for weeks and weeks. And, as is so often the case in such circumstances, the project worked: from the mysterious depths of the mind something horrendous came forth.

It was late one night roughly a month after their experiment began that Freeman went into that old, dark cellar with the intent of trying to further enhance their tulpa—and was confronted by something hideous and almost heart-stopping. To his horror, Freeman could see on one of the stone walls of the cellar a large, shadowy image. It was that of a huge spider, crawling and creeping slowly along the wall. Its eight legs and bulbous body stood out prominently. Freeman was frozen to the spot for a few moments. Fortunately though, he managed to break the spell of fear-driven paralysis that had overwhelmed and gripped him, and he quietly and carefully backed up the stairs and exited the room—being sure to lock it behind him.

Clearly, the fact that the spider was only seen in the form of a shadow suggests that while the process of raising a tulpa version of Atlach-Nacha was certainly working, it was going to take much more work to ensure that the creature became fully formed. That was destined not to happen, though. Worried about the possibility that they really had opened the genie's bottle, so to speak, the group of friends decided that something had to be done. They chose to end the experiment, lest it spiral wildly out of control. It was probably a very wise move. The altar was destroyed, as was the web-like cloth. And, most important of all, the friends did their best not to think about Atlach-Nacha, which, admittedly, was not exactly the easiest thing for them to do. Evidently, though, the process worked and the tulpa was exterminated before it had the chance to attain a greater sense of reality and wreak who knows how much untold havoc.

Now it's time to look at the tulpa version of a comic book hero.

A Comic Book Creation Becomes Much More

Alan Moore is an acclaimed comic book writer and the man who was responsible for *Watchmen* and *V for Vendetta*—both of which were made into hit movies. Then there is John Constantine, Moore's most loved and popular character from the 1980s. The character became a hit on the big screen in 2005 when the well-received movie *Constantine* was released in cinemas on a worldwide scale.

It wasn't long at all after the Constantine character came to fruition in Alan Moore's mind that Moore encountered Constantine in what was without much doubt a tulpa form. It was an otherwise normal day in London, England, and Moore was eating lunch in a café in Westminster, when none other than John Constantine—the comic book creation of Moore himself—walked right past him. In Moore's own words, which are cited in Jim McGrath's online blog, in a post called "Conjuring Constantine" from August 2012, "He looked exactly like John Constantine. He looked at me, stared me straight in the eyes, smiled, nodded almost conspiratorially, and then just walked off around the corner to the other part of the snack bar."

With his nerves jangled to a major degree, Moore debated whether or not he should follow his creation come to life. Moore chose not to. It's almost certainly not a coincidence, given the nature of the strange affair, that Moore is not just a comic book writer. He is also a practicing chaos magician. It just so happens that chaos magic involves the conjuring and creating of fictional characters, giving them some semblance of reality.

Subconsciously, one suspects this is exactly what Moore did: he created a temporary tulpa of John Constantine. And having done so, Moore was duly paid a visit of a truly extraordinary kind. Perhaps, had the story been spread far and wide, causing belief in the Constantine tulpa to take off big-time, we would have seen the entity feeding on that collective belief and thriving very nicely. That it was not seen again, however, is a good indication that its life was destined to be a short one, a life that could not be sustained because of a lack of strong enough belief.

The Skinny on the Slenderman

There is very little doubt that the most powerful tulpa in today's world is the Slenderman, an internet sensation that is part Man in Black, part ghoul, and part Lovecraftian nightmare. The story of the pale, faceless, black-suited, tentacle-waving monster dates back to 2009. That was the year in which a man named Eric Knudsen created the Slenderman—purely as a piece of entertainment and nothing more—for the Something Awful website. Knudsen skillfully manipulated a couple of black-and-white photos and inserted his creepy creation into them, showing the Slenderman among groups of children—whom, in the tales, he preys upon in disturbing fashion.

In no time at all, certainly surprising Eric Knudsen, the Slenderman went from being a bit of harmless, net-based fun to a full-blown meme: blogs were created in his name, fictional stories were posted online to further expand the legend of the creature, and his devoted following of largely young children and teenagers grew at a phenomenal and extraordinary rate.

The entertainment angle was most definitely eclipsed in 2014 when, on May 31, two twelve-year-old girls from Waukesha, Wisconsin, attacked and almost killed a former school friend. She was stabbed close to twenty times in a frenzied and furious attack. It was all done in the name of the Slenderman, who the two girls believed would allow them entry into his spooky mansion in the woods as a result of their planned sacrifice. Thankfully, the girl who was attacked survived and made a full recovery. Both of the girls who committed the attack plead guilty, but were found not guilty on grounds of mental illness.

When the story of the attack got out, it became not just local or even national news; it became worldwide news. The result was that millions of people had now heard of the Slenderman. And guess what happened. That's right: the Slenderman began to be seen in the real world. Eric Knudsen's internet creation had—just like Richard Freeman's spider god and Alan Moore's John Constantine—come to life in the form of a tulpa. The massive belief that so many kids had in the Slenderman allowed it to take hold of our reality. The Slenderman didn't just dine on belief—it totally *feasted* on it. *Gorged* might be an even better word to use.

Since the events of 2014, witnesses claim to have seen the Slenderman in their bedrooms in the dead of night—which is the Slenderman's typical time to surface and hunt. Others have heard it calling to them on their laptops and iPhones. More than a few have encountered it in dark and shadowy woods, which is the preferred area for the Slenderman to lurk in. There are even accounts of the Slenderman invading and manipulating people's dreams and turning them into full-blown nightmares.

To say that the Slenderman is the definitive tulpa is not wrong; in fact, it's right on the money. Its massive following has ensured that. And right now there doesn't appear to be any way to deconstruct the tulpa version of Eric Knudsen's creation, such is its immense power. By feeding on the beliefs of what may easily amount to millions of kids, the Slenderman is all but indestructible. And, of course, while it is very easy to think about the Slenderman, it's extremely difficult *not* to think about it—particularly so when the matter is placed in your mind, which is what I have just done to you, the reader. In fact, just by reading these very words, you may be inadvertently making the Slenderman tulpa more powerful by the moment, as it voraciously devours belief upon belief.

When Emotions Run Wild

Related to the phenomenon of the tulpa is that of the poltergeist. The word itself is German, but in English it means "noisy spirit." The poltergeist is a dangerous and violent entity that engages in hostile activity, torments those in the home where the activity is taking place, and can place the victims of its attacks in downright danger. The poltergeist is somewhat different from the average disembodied spirit, however. Faced with the likes of furniture moving across one's living room, windows shattering, beds raising off the floor, books flying off their shelves, and electrical items blowing out, it's perfectly natural to ascribe all of this chilling activity to an evil, supernatural entity. Things aren't quite as straightforward as that, however, which you'll now see.

It's a fact that the vast majority of all poltergeist activity revolves around one particular person in the targeted family. Typically, it's a young girl—either prepubescent or going through puberty. One particular school of thought suggests that certain supernatural entities are attracted to young girls. That does not appear to be the case when it comes to the issue of poltergeists, though. In an article titled "Poltergeists," the Crystalinks website states, "Due to hormonal and emotional changes in the teenager's body, negative energy may be thrust outwardly sometimes moving or destroying objects telekinetically."

In other words, what we have here is a case of young girls unknowingly causing the very phenomena that we assume have external components dictating and directing them—such as a ghost, a demon, or perhaps even one of the Shadow People. On rare occasions, the girl may spontaneously manifest the image of a ghostly figure—albeit not from some hellish, unearthly realm, but from the depths of her dark imagination and subconscious. And the greater the level of that "negative energy" that Crystalinks refers to, the greater the power and substance that is given to that creation of the imagination.

So, what we have here is a chaotic, spiraling situation. It begins in the throes of the mind, but can rapidly become externalized in just about the worst ways conceivable. As for the causal factor—the young girl—she typically finds herself feeling weaker and weaker as the incidents and experiences grow in number. It's no wonder. The girl is unknowingly discharging precious human energy into her immediate environment—energy that she cannot do without. The result is exactly what we have seen in so many other examples in this book—the central person in the saga gets sick and weak as the freakish phenomena increase.

In essence, the girl is destroying her very own health by expelling the essential energies that her body requires— energies which then wreak havoc in the home. Fortunately, in many cases, poltergeist activity will come to a sudden halt after a period of days, weeks, or even months. Why? Maybe because the hormonal imbalances that we all go through in puberty have leveled out in the involved young person, and the turmoil and emotional highs and lows have begun to lessen. As they lessen, so does the amount of energy directed to keeping the poltergeist "alive"—to the point where, finally, the energy has dissipated and the poltergeist is no more.

8
THE DJINN

Of all the energy-based supernatural entities that see us as their food, none are more feared and revered—in equal amounts—than the Middle Eastern djinn. They are ancient and powerful beings that should be avoided at all costs. Although at times they can be friendly and helpful, the djinn are also dangerous and manipulative—just like so many other paranormal parasites that need us as a form of sustenance. Without a doubt, one of the most learned researchers in the field of energy-based entities is Rosemary Ellen Guiley, whose books include *The Vengeful Djinn* and *The Djinn Connection*. In an online article titled "Facts About the Djinn," Guiley says this of their strange feeding habits:

> They can eat human food when they take human form, but our food does not sustain them. It gives them

pleasure. They can absorb the essence of food, and things like the molecules from tobacco smoke, which provide enjoyment. Their main source of nourishment is the absorption of energy from life forms. The best is the draining of a soul, but is difficult to do and is considered unlawful. It is, however, practiced by certain powerful, renegade Djinn. The vampiric absorption of the life force can be quite detrimental to people, and cause health problems.

With that all said, before we get to the matter of how and why the djinn need us, and the particular nature of the energy they absorb from us, let's first take a look at the history of these enigmatic, powerful creatures and our uneasy relationship.

From Satan to Shaitan

According to ancient lore, the djinn existed long before we did—tens of thousands of years before us, in fact. The story of the djinn is detailed in the pages of the Quran. It is the sacred book of Islamic teachings, which those of the Muslim faith believe is the word of God—or Allah, as he is known in their religion. Although there are significant differences between the Bible and the Quran, there are a lot of deep similarities, too. The Bible teaches that God created the human race, in the form of Adam and Eve, Eve having allegedly been crafted from one of Adam's ribs. In the world of Islam, Allah brought Adam into being, too. But he did much more than that. As well as bringing the human race and the angels to life, Allah also created supernatural entities that, in terms of power and stature, were right up there with the angels. They were, if you have not already guessed, the mighty djinn of old.

Things went wrong for the djinn—drastically so—when Allah insisted that they display deep reverence for Adam. The angels were ordered to do likewise. And while the angels dutifully did what they were told, the djinn most assuredly did not. They chose to vehemently go against the word of Allah. For the djinn, this proved to be utterly disastrous: they were unceremoniously flung out of the realm of heaven. Their only chance of retaining some degree of their original, powerful status is when judgment day finally comes along. That, we are told, is when all of the djinn will be placed before Allah and given the opportunity to make things right. Until then, and under the law of Allah, the djinn are free to do as they please—which includes feeding on us and, if they choose, even forever obliterating us from existence. While the djinn can—to a degree—encourage people to perform sinful acts, they cannot literally force us to commit murder and violence. We are still very much the deciders.

The mightiest of all the djinn is Iblis. In fact, he is the overlord of the djinn. His name translates into English as "despair." In essence, Iblis can be compared to Satan—in the sense that one of his prime directives is to lure the human race to the dark side. The parallel between the devil and Iblis is made even more obvious by the fact that in Islamic lore Iblis's alternative name is Shaitan—which only serves to amplify the satanic-themed links between Iblis and the devil of the Bible. Iblis being the ultimate djinn has given rise to the theory that the rest of the djinn hordes are the equivalents of the Bible's demons. Certainly, there are uncanny similarities between both stories.

It was Iblis himself who ordered his fellow djinn to disobey Allah's order to bow down before Adam. Iblis's argument was that he and the rest of the djinn were superior beings formed from smokeless fire, while Adam was a lowly being of nothing but mere dirt. Iblis saw himself and his kind far above the human race, when it came to the issue of stature. Iblis was right about the power of the djinn versus that of us. And unlike us, the djinn have massively long life spans. From our perspective, the djinn are practically immortal. Iblis, like all djinn, is a shape-shifting entity with the ability to take on multiple forms—including that of a large black dog, an elemental, an extraterrestrial, and a snake. The djinn can also negotiate dimensions as easily as we change channels on our televisions. So, in that sense, *yes*, the djinn *are* our superiors—and masterful manipulators of us, too.

It must be said that, today, the nature of the djinn has been hugely dumbed down—in the world of Western entertainment, they have become known as genies. The genuie an entity that most people expect to see in movies, on

TV shows, and in kids' cartoons. With its attendant three wishes, the genie is seen as a wholly mythical, harmless, magical thing. The truth, however, is just about as far away from that image as it's possible to get. Forget Aladdin and his lamp: the true djinn are among the most fearsome—and fearless—entities that can intrude on our world and wreak havoc and mayhem as they see fit. Let's take a closer look at the lives and domains of these unearthly things.

The Mysteries of Plasma

One of the most intriguing things about the djinn is that, as we have seen, they were born out of smokeless fire. But how could a form of fire feed on human energy, and have intelligence, a physical form, and the ability to manipulate our minds? Well, the answer is simple: fire just cannot perform the incredible feats that the djinn are said to carry out. In all likelihood, the reference to the djinn having their origins in fire is a distortion. But of what? Rosemary Ellen Guiley believes she knows. It all revolves around something called *plasma.*

For those who may not know what exactly plasma is, consider the words of the Southwest Research Institute (SRI) on the nature of plasma, from an article titled "Plasma: The Fourth State of Matter":

> A plasma is a hot ionized gas consisting of approximately equal numbers of positively charged ions and negatively charged electrons. The

characteristics of plasmas are significantly different from those of ordinary neutral gases so that plasmas are considered a distinct 'fourth state of matter.'

The Illinois-based Qualitative Reasoning Group of Northwestern University states the following in "What is plasma?":

Plasma is a cloud of protons, neutrons and electrons where all the electrons have come loose from their respective molecules and atoms, giving the plasma the ability to act as a whole rather than as a bunch of atoms. A plasma is more like a gas than any of the other states of matter because the atoms are not in constant contact with each other, but it behaves differently from a gas. It has what scientists call collective behavior. This means that the plasma can flow like a liquid or it can contain areas that are like clumps of atoms sticking together.

Rosemary Ellen Guiley believes—and is probably correct in her conclusions—that the djinn are plasma-based entities, which in all likelihood led to the distorted legend that they were the product of fire. She also concludes that the hellish and heavenly realms described in the Bible and the Quran were really dimensions of existence very different from our 3-D reality.

In a December 2014 article written for Phys.org and titled "A universe of 10 dimensions," Matt Williams says that aside from our three dimensions, "scientists believe that there may be many more. In fact, the theoretical framework of superstring theory posits that the universe exists in ten different dimensions. These different aspects are what govern the universe, the fundamental forces of nature, and all the elementary particles contained within."

Might such realms as heaven and hell really be two of many more dimensions beyond ours? Don't bet against it. And don't bet against the idea that the djinn also inhabit such realms, but in the form of plasma, rather than flesh, blood, and bone.

The Lives of the Djinn

Ancient lore tells us that although the djinn are very different from us—certainly in terms of their makeup—they are not too dissimilar in some other ways. The world of Islam maintains that the djinn have almost unending lives—although they are not literally immortal. Not even the djinn can beat the reaper forever. They marry, they have offspring, and, like us, there are both male and female djinn.

Although the mysterious planes of existence that the djinn inhabit are very different from ours, the actual space they inhabit is the same. In other words, you could be sitting at home, reading a book, and not realize that you are being eyed carefully by a dangerous djinn that has invaded your space, and can see your every move, but that is effectively still within its very own dimension. When they leave their dimensional planes and enter our domain, the djinn are said to dwell in caves, in deep and winding tunnels, and in the remains of crumbled, old structures—particularly in the heart of the Middle East. And it's in the early hours of the morning when they are most active in our world.

Also like us, the djinn love music: singing and whistling are two of their primary ways of entertaining themselves. If you wake in the middle of the night and you hear disembodied whistling or the vague tones of faraway enchanting and hypnotic music you may well have a djinn in your abode. They prefer Middle Eastern music and that of ancient India, too—particularly the sound of a sitar. The djinn are also said to love dogs, which reportedly can see them even when we can't, as can donkeys.

The djinns' love of dogs mostly does not extend to us, though. However, they will, on occasion, offer the targets of their torture a gift, a goal, or good fortune. Almost certainly, this is where the tales of the "three wishes" originated—with an ancient knowledge and tradition that one could make a deal with the djinn. Like most such pacts, though, it's very seldom that anything good ever comes from them. The djinn also have the ability to intrude on and even enter the minds of those they target. Essentially, we're talking about something akin to demonic possession. People can be made to perform all manner of terrible acts that might be put down as mental illness or the result of an evil, psychopathic mind. That might not be the case, though: the person may be used as a vessel by the djinn. Why? Because the djinn enjoy manipulating and tormenting us—it really is that simple. And terrifying too.

On occasion, the djinn will not exhibit dangerous or even deadly behavior. Sometimes, their actions are solely manipulative—even bordering on what almost amounts to game playing. They may move a household item to a new place, baffling people as to how such a thing has happened. They can command electricity—even thunderstorms. They may cause your microwave oven to explode. Your phone may briefly fail to work—right at the same time that you hear that curious whistling in your home. Screwing around with us—for no good reason beyond the fact they get some form of delight out of it all—is at the heart of what motivates the djinns' interactions with us. Illness—both mental and physical—typifies encounters with the djinn, too.

And none of us should forget the warning words of Rosemary Ellen Guiley on the matter of the djinn: "Their main source of nourishment is the absorption of energy from life forms."

On this latter point from Rosemary Ellen Guiley, it's worth noting the experience of Emily. Her 1999 encounter with a shadowy entity in her San Antonio, Texas, apartment is highly suggestive of an interaction with a djinn—possibly even several. That Emily became fascinated by the djinn phenomenon just a few weeks before very strange activity began in her home is another pointer suggesting that by both reading and thinking about the djinn, she opened the kind of doorway that most of us would prefer stayed shut.

Emily says that only days into reading a second book on the djinn, she began to see—out of the corners of her eyes—small, shadow-like figures lurking behind the corners of the couch, peering from behind doorways, and even tugging on the duvet of her bed at night. She experienced endless electricity outages, and her microwave stopped working, as did the electric alarm clock in her bedroom. On top of that, Emily had several nightmares of a djinn, in which the creature sucked the energy out of her in a mouth-to-mouth fashion—almost as if the djinn was kissing the energy out of her, which is exactly how Emily described it. A spine-tingling image, to be sure.

9
SOUL STEALERS

There can be very few people who are interested in the domain of the supernatural who have not heard of the so-called alien abduction phenomenon. It's a subject that has captured the attention of not just UFO enthusiasts, but also the mainstream media and the public, too. To demonstrate how the subject has become part of the mainstream, one only has to take a look at the story of Whitley Strieber's 1987 book, *Communion*. In no time at all, Strieber's book—which told of his very own encounters with abductors that he called "the Visitors"—became a *New York Times* bestseller. Such a thing was previously unheard of in the domain of ufology. On top of that, Strieber and his late wife, Anne, received quite literally hundreds of thousands of letters from the readers of *Communion*, all wanting to share their own personal stories. Clearly, the phenomenon resonates with people to an extraordinarily high degree.

It's hard to say with 100 percent certainty when the first alien abduction event occurred. Many early encounters may never have been revealed, chiefly due to concerns and fears of ridicule. There is, however, no doubt at all about which case was responsible for bringing the issue to a wide audience. It was a curious affair that occurred on the night of September 19, 1961, and was chronicled at length in John Fuller's very appropriately titled book from 1966, *The Interrupted Journey*. The story revolves around a married couple, Barney and Betty Hill, from New Hampshire. They had taken what promised to be a welcoming vacation to Canada. It was. The pair had a great time; one of the highlights was a trip to Niagara Falls. It was on the way back home, however, that everything went wrong and their lives rapidly unraveled.

Strangers in the Night

All was normal until, on one particularly dark stretch of road near Lincoln, New Hampshire, the Hills saw something strange in the black skies above them. What it was, Betty and Barney had no idea. But it certainly didn't look like a regular aircraft or helicopter, that's for sure. They were particularly attracted by "its shape and the intensity of its lighting as compared to the stars in the sky," reported Major Paul W. Henderson, of the US Air Force, in an official dossier on the incident—dated September 21, 1961—which has been declassified under the terms of the US Freedom of Information Act.

So amazed by what they were seeing, Betty and Barney stopped their car and they got out to take a closer look at it with Barney's binoculars, which he had fortunately brought along on the vacation. The object—perhaps reacting to the actions of the pair—shot away, performing erratic maneuvers, constantly changing its flight pattern, and even briefly hovering silently in the sky. Then something even more incredible happened: what appeared to be a pair of wings came out of the craft, which gave the vehicle an appearance that was somewhat airplane-like. According to Major Henderson, in his aforementioned report, the pair saw the craft "swoop down in the general direction of their auto." As the UFO closed in, both husband and wife could now hear a curious series of "buzzes" coming from it. The object soon shot away again and the Hills, amazed and more than a bit alarmed over what had happened, couldn't do much beyond continue with their drive. Interestingly, although they did not see the craft again, they did hear the odd "buzz" once more—this time when they were in the area of Ashland, roughly thirty miles from Lincoln.

While that, in essence, is what the Hills consciously remembered, there was also the matter of what was deeply buried within the minds of Betty and Barney—which they *couldn't* remember, at least not consciously. In the days and weeks after the event, both Betty and Barney began to experience traumatic and frightening dreams—of not just seeing a UFO, but also of being taken on board and essentially being treated like lab rats. They were subjected to a number of trauma-filled experiments—which included Betty having a needle painfully pushed into her navel. It sounds vaguely like an amniocentesis test, but it was clearly something else, as during an amniocentesis procedure, the needle is inserted into the wall of the abdomen, finally reaching the amniotic sac. When the nightmares grew ever worse for the Hills, and continued for no less than a couple of years, the pair knew that they finally had to do something about it. In doing so, they alerted the world to the alien abduction phenomenon—although that was certainly not their intention.

When Time Vanishes

In December 1963, Barney and Betty decided to consult a Massachusetts-based psychiatrist and neurologist named Benjamin Simon. A wealth of hypnotic sessions soon followed, which showed that the Hills had experienced a significant amount of what, in UFO research, is known as "missing time." Something very strange had taken place on the drive home, something which finally led the Hills to the conclusion that alien entities had wiped their memories clean of what really happened on that dark September night in 1961. Such was the interest in the case—since back then it was largely unique in the field of ufology, which had focused on UFO research rather than abductions since it began in the 1940s—that it led John Fuller to pen *The Interrupted Journey*. The alien abduction phenomenon was born. It not only continues to live, it positively thrives. And on a worldwide basis, too.

Since the now-historic encounter of Betty and Barney Hill in September 1961, literally thousands of alien abduction cases have been reported all across the globe. How many cases remain completely *un*reported—for fear of ridicule or of being labeled a liar or a crank—is anyone's guess. There is, however, one aspect of the alien abduction controversy that most assuredly does not get the coverage that it deserves. It is an issue that involves the syphoning and even the *ingesting* of the human soul—by apparently soulless creatures from some other realm of existence. It's an aspect of the UFO phenomenon that takes us down an avenue far removed from the conventional image of flying saucers and little green men.

Death's Door and a Nuclear Nightmare

Many UFO researchers are reluctant to address the "aliens are eating our souls" theory. The fact is, though, that there are far more than a few such reports on record. In fact, it's fair and accurate to say there are an incredible number of such cases. However, the problem is that for so many in ufology, the subject is so troubling and disturbing that they choose to outright ignore it. Before we get to the "eating" angle, let's first make a case that there is indeed a connection between the alien abduction issue and the human soul. You may be surprised by the scale of such encounters.

One of the earliest—and most intriguing—cases on record came from a man named Paul Inglesby. Just one year before the Second World War broke out in 1939, Inglesby—who died in 2010—came down with a very serious case of malaria. So serious was it that for a while Inglesby perilously hovered in that mysterious domain between life and death. It was while in this limbo state that Inglesby had a frightening dream.

Years later, he recalled how it all went down: It was an undetermined time in the earth's future and UFO-like craft were soaring across the fire and smoke filled skies of our ruined, radioactive planet and launching nuclear missiles at our major cities—killing billions and causing planetwide destruction. The UFOs were not piloted by extraterrestrials, though, but by demonic entities whose goal was to suck out the souls of those killed in the fiery inferno, which was rapidly overwhelming the earth and just about everything on it.

For Inglesby, it was quite literally a wake-up call. The malaria cleared up, Inglesby came out of his unconscious state, and he spent the rest of his life pursuing a career in the church and warning people to avoid the UFO issue. He feared that it would lead people to become ensnared by malevolent demonic monsters, all of which he warned people of in his 1978 book, *UFOs and the Christian*.

"I Think We're Property"

The unsettling story of Paul Inglesby dates back to the 1930s, but it was in the 1950s that he largely began talking about his nightmare—after he realized that what he had seen back in 1938 were images of nuclear explosions and "mushroom clouds," the type that were all too familiar by the 1950s. It's important to note, though, that a connection between UFOs, aliens, and the human soul didn't really surface to any kind of meaningful degree until the latter part of the 1980s—which takes us back to the issue of Whitley Strieber's bestseller of 1987, *Communion*.

When word of Strieber's planned book first got out, most ufologists assumed that the book, in terms of its content and its theories, would be fairly akin to John Fuller's *The Interrupted Journey* of 1966 and Budd Hopkins's 1981 book, *Missing Time*. Both books adhered to the now-familiar theory that aliens are stealing our DNA to save their waning species. Well, they are certainly stealing *something*, but it's not our DNA. Strieber's revelations were, in many respects, far removed from the writings of Hopkins and Fuller, which is why the book created such a firestorm in locales where ufologists hang out.

In *Communion*, Strieber made it very clear that his own encounters with the Visitors—and those of others he had spoken to—revealed a startling connection between alien abductions and the human soul, a paradigm-shifting connection. In his book, Strieber talked about how abductees experienced their souls being "dragged" from their bodies during abductions. Strieber himself was told by his abductors that they "recycled" human souls. That sounds quite comforting, as it suggests reincarnation may be a reality—something which will ensure us further lives after this one. But was Strieber being told the entire truth by his captors?

Or was this an attempt on their part to use lies to push things down a different, more appealing path?

Strieber said that the more and more he dug into the matter of his encounters, and as he tried to get a handle on what was afoot, he was unable to banish Charles Fort's theories from his mind. For those who may not know, Fort was an acclaimed writer on all manner of paranormal phenomena. His books included *Lo!* and *Wild Talents*. In Strieber's 1988 book, *Transformation*, he specifically quotes Fort's dark suggestion that we, the human race, are "animals here for the slaughter and incapable of seeing the greater and more terrible meanings that surround us."

As for more of Charles Fort's opinions, they can be read in his classic title from 1919, *The Book of the Damned*. In it, Fort writes, "I think we're property. I should say we belong to something: That once upon a time, this earth was No-man's Land, that other worlds explored and colonized here, and fought among themselves for possession, but that now it's owned by something: That something owns this earth—all others warned off."

As If I Was Dead in My Bed

Whitley Strieber is not the only writer-researcher on the alien abduction issue to have made a deep connection between the phenomenon and the human soul. Another was the late Dr. John E. Mack, a Harvard University professor who was killed by a drunk driver in London in 2004. Mack wrote two books on the subject, *Abduction* and *Passport to the Cosmos*. One of Mack's many patients was a man named Greg. He told Mack of an experience of the abduction type—but not with the typical small, large-headed, black-eyed aliens that have become known as the Greys. No, Greg's encounter was with tall, scaly creatures that resembled the monster in Universal's classic movie of 1954, *The Creature from the Black Lagoon*. In UFO terminology, they are known as the Reptilians. Greg confided in Mack that he felt the lizard people he encountered were trying to extract his soul from his physical body. Another of Mack's patients, Isabel, spoke of aliens that could "fool you into handing over" your soul.

It's also worth noting the experience of Sergeant John Healey of the US Army Reserve. On the night of October 18, 1973, he encountered a brightly lit UFO, as he and his colleagues were on board a UH-1 helicopter, rapidly closing in on Cleveland Hopkins Airport, Ohio. In the aftermath of the encounter—which, in essence, was a near collision between the two crafts—Healey had several weird out-of-body experiences, which he told UFO investigator Jennie Zeidman about. It was, he explained, as if he was dead in his bed and his spirit was above him, staring down at his sleeping form in the bed. That Sergeant Healey's experiences occurred not in relation to the abduction phenomenon, but to a UFO sighting, suggests that other components of the UFO issue come into play regarding the relationship between UFOs, life after death, and our souls. Notably, several members of the helicopter crew were later contacted by representatives of the Department of Defense, who exhibited interest in and deep concerns about the UFO/soul-ingestion angle. This suggests a disturbing scenario: that certain elements of the US government may know something about the origins and agenda of the paranormal parasites. In fact, as we'll now see, that's exactly how it seems. Uncle Sam may know all about these menacing energy-eating entities that intrude upon our world.

A Whistleblower More Controversial than Edward Snowden? Yes!

Now let's take a look at the incredible story of a man named Robert Scott Lazar, who prefers to go by Bob. For several months in the latter part of 1988, Lazar was employed at the most famous and mysterious US government–owned facility of all time—Area 51—which is located in the depths of the Nevada desert. Specifically, Lazar worked in a portion of the facility called S-4. The origins of the base date back to the early 1950s, when the incredibly well-guarded installation was constructed to oversee the testing of new and radical aircraft. Over the years, the U-2 spy plane, SR-71 Blackbird spy plane, and both the F-117 Nighthawk stealth fighter and B-2 Spirit stealth bomber were all tested and secretly flown at Area 51. All with practically no one—outside of the programs—ever having any idea of what was taking place. Area 51 is surely the ultimate modern-day fortress.

As most people will be aware, Area 51 is far more well-known for the tales coming out of the base in relation to UFOs and aliens. So the story goes, since the 1950s Area 51 has been the secret storage area—and possibly even the testing area—for an untold number of captured or crashed and recovered extraterrestrial spacecraft. Some are said to be partially wrecked and others, we are told, are in near-pristine conditions. There is no doubt that without the testimony that surfaced publicly from Lazar in early 1989—when he spoke with George Knapp, of Las Vegas's KLAS-TV, who devoted significant airtime to the words of the controversial whistleblower—Area 51 would still languish in secrecy and obscurity, unknown to just about one and all. Lazar told Knapp that programs were actively running at Area 51 to try to understand the extraterrestrial technology that was in the hands of the US government's finest and most brilliant scientists. Lazar continued, saying that a small team at the base was trying to duplicate the technology and that, incredibly, there might have been both dead and *living* aliens at the base—the latter dwelling deep underground, amid a myriad of tunnels and caverns way below the desert environment of Nevada.

Although the US government will not confirm Lazar's claims of alien activity at Area 51—which is not at all surprising—it's most intriguing and telling that the government also refuses to deny the story. Instead, the government has done nothing but offer a stony, awkward silence. Had Lazar concocted the whole thing out of his own mind, one could make a good argument that it would have been very easy for officialdom to quickly bring matters to rest. But, three decades after Lazar came forward, there is still no denunciation from the government. Sometimes, silence speaks volumes—and that may be the case in regard to Lazar and his claims of extensive UFO activity at Area 51.

Now, let's take a look at what Lazar learned during his brief time at Area 51, in relation to the matter of the human soul. It adds further support to the theory that the government knows, or suspects, what the soul eaters want from us. In addition, it provides a good, solid reason why the government may be fearful of sharing the terrifying facts with the rest of us.

"We're Containers"

It's important to note that Bob Lazar was only in the employ of Area 51 for several months. There was a very good reason for that: When he was initially offered the job, Lazar was specifically warned that speaking out of turn on what was afoot at the base would be absolutely unacceptable—possibly even dangerous to his life. Lazar, however, being something of a self-confessed maverick, chose to ignore this direct, stern order. Instead, Lazar quietly told his wife and a good friend named Gene Huff what was going on at Area 51: aliens, UFOs, the whole show in fact. When Lazar learned that his phone was being monitored and that his bosses at the base knew he had spilled the beans—and, as a result, were angry in the extreme—he decided never to go back to the base, fearing that if he did he might not get out alive. Lazar's bones just might have ended up buried somewhere in the Nevada desert. His suspicions might have been right on target. So, in essence, it was Lazar himself who terminated his own employment—rather than being terminated in a very different and fatal way.

In that roughly three months of employment, Lazar learned a great deal—all of it amazing and life-changing. Had he not quit the program out of a deep concern for his safety, Lazar would likely have learned even more. According to the man himself, he was briefed on the long and winding history of the alien presence on earth. He was told that the aliens were responsible for the creation and development of all of the world's major religions, and that the extraterrestrial creatures came from a faraway star system.

More controversially, the aliens had supposedly genetically altered various kinds of early humans—such as the Neanderthals and the Cro-Magnons—into what we, *Homo sapiens*, are today. None of this, Lazar was told, could ever be shared with the public, due to the catastrophic effect it would have on the world of religion and the stability of human civilization. It was, the staff at Area 51 said, just too difficult and dangerous a story to share. Risking worldwide shock and even the collapse of civilization was simply not in the cards. So, the keepers of the secrets at Area 51 chose to tell no one outside of the program—*ever*.

There was something else, too, that Lazar learned from the top secret briefing papers showed to him at Area 51. In fact, it was probably the most controversial aspect of his entire story.

Of all the various revelations that Lazar made, the one—more than any other—that disturbed and troubled him, was in regard to the human soul. The government was hiding, out at Area 51, something that amounted to just about the biggest secret of all. Lazar learned that the aliens supposedly refer to us, the human race, as "containers." Containers of what? Containers of souls, that's what. On this issue, Lazar told George Knapp, on Las Vegas's KLAS-TV in 1989, that "religion was created so we have some rules and regulations for the sole purpose of not damaging the containers."

George Knapp was not the only person whom Bob Lazar spoke to on this issue of containers. Michael Lindemann is the editor of a 1995 book, *UFOs and the Alien Presence*. He also questioned Lazar on this controversy. Lazar added a bit more to the story when speaking with Lindemann, as the latter acknowledged in his book. He noted that Lazar said the containers were "extremely, extremely unique," that they were "very difficult to find," and that the biggest secret of all revolved around our souls. No wonder that the people in the know at Area 51 didn't know how to tell the rest of the world the story they were forced to sit on—out of fear of worldwide anarchy breaking out if it was revealed that religion was a creation of ancient extraterrestrials who devour our souls.

But what is it that is so important about the human soul, and how does it come into play with the story that this book tells? Let's see.

Faustian Pacts and *The Matrix*

Ray Boeche is both a priest and a UFO researcher who believes that the UFO phenomenon is demonic—rather than extraterrestrial—in nature. In November 1991, Boeche met with two Department of Defense physicists who were playing a dangerous game, an *incredibly* dangerous game. They were part of a top-secret program working out of the Pentagon, which was focused on contacting what were referred to by the group as "Non-Human Entities," or NHEs. The plan was for the US government to try to make what we might call a "deal" with the NHEs—to specifically try to understand, replicate, and then weaponize the supernatural powers of the demonic NHEs.

Of course, the whole plan went totally awry—as Faustian pacts *always* do. There were deaths on the program, runs of bad luck, and a sense that the group had somehow been cursed—which was probably right on target. The two officials that Boeche met with wanted his guidance—as a prominent figure in the church, and also as someone well-affiliated with the UFO phenomenon—on what they should do next. Not surprisingly, Boeche said that nothing good or positive could come from engaging the NHEs. They should be completely avoided at all costs, he said. The two men thanked him and went on their way. Boeche had a couple more communications with them, after which there was nothing but a stony silence. The group still exists, though.

Thanks to Ray Boeche sharing his story with me in January 2007, I was able to meet with a small number of those who were still working on the program. One of the many things I was told by the group members very much ties in with what Bob Lazar talked about, as well as the observations of Professor John E. Mack, Paul Inglesby, and Whitley Strieber: namely, that the human soul was at the heart of the UFO presence on earth.

They believe that this was all a distortion of the real story—which was very different from the conventional story of hell, the devil, and his minions. The program concluded something that is all but guaranteed to give each and every one of us nightmares: that the human soul is, in essence, a form of supernatural energy—a form of energy that the NHEs *digest*, rather than torment at the will of the devil. The bleak conclusion of those in the know in the Pentagon was that our souls are the food of the NHEs. This, you will recall, harks back to the comments of both Whitley Strieber and Charles Fort, who drew parallels between the earth and a farm, with us as the cattle caught in the middle.

It's a story not unlike that presented in the 1999 movie *The Matrix*. In the film, the human race is nothing but a source of fuel for highly advanced machines that thrive on our electrical energy, while we all unknowingly live in a dream world born out of a sophisticated hologram—the matrix of the movie's title. Our lives are one big, collective nightmare, while the reality is the hellish matrix. Just perhaps, the fiction of *The Matrix* is not as far removed from the truth as many might suspect it to be.

We'll close this chapter with the words of a man named Nigel Kerner, who has put together a persuasive argument that it is the human soul which obsessively attracts the Greys of alien abduction lore to us. Kerner has written two books on this very topic: *The Song of the Greys*, which was published in 1997, and 2010's *Grey Aliens and the Harvesting of Souls*. Kerner concludes that, essentially, the Greys are biological robots, created entities that lack the one thing we all have: a soul. For that reason, they are determined to make use of the human soul in much the same way we do: as a vessel to ensure that they live on after physical, bodily death. Kerner says on his website, "these entities are attempting to 'piggy back' our facility as human beings for eternal existence, hence their apparent fascination with the human reproductive capacity."

In that sense, the agenda of the Greys may be twofold: to harness the human soul for immortality, but also to use it as a source of energy. Either way or both ways, it's fair to say we're screwed.

10
ALIENS AND ABDUCTIONS

It's not at all an exaggeration to say that some of the most disturbing stories concerning the parasitic nature of certain supernatural entities revolve around the issue of aliens and UFOs. It is within the domain of extraterrestrial life that we see a host of deeply troubling stories which may well have been covered up by government agencies, chiefly to prevent public panic on a massive scale if the truth became known. The UFO phenomenon is very much a multifaceted one: it consists of alien abductions, crop circles, UFO landing cases, close encounters, interactions between humans and extraterrestrials, Men in Black reports, military dogfights with UFOs, and much more. There is, however, another aspect to the UFO issue that often gets swept under the carpet. There is an acutely good reason for that: very few people—in government and in the field of ufology—know how to handle it. Or even if it *can* be successfully handled. It revolves around the nightmarish angle of aliens eating us.

There are solid reasons to believe that the UFO phenomenon has its dark side—an extremely dark side. We'll start with the strange, almost sci-fi-like saga of a small town in northern New Mexico that is at the very heart of this troubling situation.

Horrors in and under New Mexico

Dulce is a pleasant and inviting town that is situated in New Mexico's Rio Arriba County. It's a small town of less than three thousand people, around thirteen square miles in size. It was founded in the latter part of the nineteenth century and today is the home of the Jicarilla Apache Nation. There is nothing particularly unusual or out of the ordinary about Dulce—at least not at first glance. Look a little bit closer, though, and you'll find yourself in a world filled with dark secrets and terrifying tales of the cosmic and conspiratorial kind. And by closer, I mean below your feet—*way* below your feet—maybe even *miles* down.

Since the late 1970s, rumors have swirled to the effect that deep within the massive Archuleta Mesa that dominates the town there is a secret and futuristic facility that has been out of bounds to the US government since 1979. Today it's said that the installation is under the complete control of hostile and deadly extraterrestrials—the so-called Greys of

UFO lore—dwarfish, black-eyed, large-headed entities that are practically part of popular culture.

So the story goes that in 1979 a violent confrontation between military personnel and the aliens broke out—and we were the losers. The base, which was once a hub of human-alien interaction, is now theirs—and theirs alone. Witnesses talk of people going missing and of vast, cavern-like rooms in which people are devoured by voraciously hungry aliens. Are the tales true? How did the rumors begin? Let's take a trip back in time to the mid-to-late 1970s.

Paul Bennewitz was a scientist who, at the time, ran a company in Albuquerque called Thunder Scientific—a company that quite literally backed up onto the well-guarded fences of Kirtland Air Force Base. It was around 1978 that Bennewitz—who had a preexisting interest in UFOs—began to hear of more and more so-called alien abduction events in and around Albuquerque and farther up into northern New Mexico. On top of that, strange signals were picked up by Bennewitz on his radio equipment. He saw weird-looking aircraft soaring silently across the skies over Kirtland late at night and in the early hours of the morning. He was given accounts of abductees being secretly taken to Kirtland and grilled by US intelligence agents, who were deeply concerned about the growing number of people seemingly being kidnapped from their homes and subjected to terrifying and bizarre experiments of a genetic nature.

As the weeks and months progressed, Bennewitz came to believe something incredible: that deadly ETs were secretly getting ready to take over the planet. They were planning on doing so from their command post deep below the town of Dulce. Worldwide invasion and the enslavement of the human race were lurking just around the corner—as Bennewitz saw it, at least. Suspecting that the end really was getting nearer and nearer, Bennewitz prepared a dossier on his findings and theories. He called it "Project Beta." Bennewitz mailed copies of the controversial report to the FBI, the CIA, the NSA, every branch of the military, and even to the White House. People had to be warned—and warned now—Bennewitz wrote.

Notably, Bennewitz was not written off as a crank, as many might expect him to have been. In fact, quite the opposite was the case: intelligence agents at Kirtland Air Force Base quickly established a secret liaison with Bennewitz. They warned him about digging any further into things that could be dangerous—to his life, no less. But, those same agents also confided in Bennewitz something incredible: *that he was on the right track.* They did all they could to keep Bennewitz quiet, almost to the point of begging him to keep his mouth shut on what he knew. For Bennewitz, though, this was like a red rag to a bull. The somewhat veiled threats to keep his nose out of things only made Bennewitz push further for answers.

As an attempt to further frighten and destabilize him, US intelligence fed Bennewitz more and more faked horrific material of what was supposedly going on several miles below Dulce, including tales of the aliens using captured people—in the thousands—as food. It's no wonder—given the nature of the stories and that they were coming directly from the military—that Bennewitz became more and more paranoid. Eventually, he became completely unhinged, to the point that he ended up spending time in a local medical facility, where he was treated for stress, anxiety, and, finally, what practically amounted to a complete mental collapse. Thankfully, he recovered, but was careful to keep his distance from ufology.

Secret Experiments and Cattle Mutilations

Today, some UFO researchers dismiss Bennewitz's theories and conclusions, preferring to suspect that Bennewitz had stumbled not on alien activity, but on top-secret programs of the US military and intelligence community. By steering Bennewitz down a path filled with fictitious tales of dangerous aliens, the government would be able to divert him away from the far more down-to-earth truth, so the theory goes. On the other hand, Bennewitz, who died in 2003, still has a huge following of UFO sleuths who are absolutely certain that something abominable is going on below Dulce—and has been for years. Maybe even for *centuries*.

While Bennewitz's "Project Beta" report *does* read like something straight out of the early years of *The X-Files*, there is absolutely no doubt that Dulce itself is a very weird place, one where strange activity has been reported for years. For example, in the 1960s, the area around Dulce became the site of a classified US Atomic Energy Commission program called Gasbuggy. It was part of a larger operation codenamed Plowshare. The plan was to explode a significant lysized atomic device underground, deep below the Carson National Forest, which just happens to be only a few miles from Dulce. The reason was to try to access massive and precious supplies of natural gas. The bomb was detonated on December 10, 1967—more than four thousand feet below the surface. Although the Plowshare program continued in the area until the late 1970s, even today digging underground in the area is strictly forbidden.

In light of all of Bennewitz's findings, it's not at all surprising that there are those in the UFO community who believe that the Plowshare program was actually a cover story—one created to mask the fact that the US government tried to destroy the alien base under Dulce with a nuclear weapon. That just such a weapon really *was* detonated underground, and only a few minutes from Dulce, ensures that the rumors of an alien presence in the area continue to thrive. And the fact that people are warned not to dig underground in the area only adds to the suspicions that there is something very sinister going on below Dulce.

Beyond that, in 1989, thanks to the provisions of the Freedom of Information Act, the FBI declassified into the public domain its extensive files on so-called "cattle mutilations" in the Dulce area, all of which occurred in the 1970s. Such mutilations have been reported all across the county since 1967, but Dulce is renowned for the huge number of cases in its midst, as the FBI learned.

Cattle are found lacking major organs. Blood is removed from the bodies in astonishingly quick time. And black and unmarked helicopters are seen in the areas of mutilation—as are strange lights in the sky and UFOs, too.

Incredibly, all of these issues are discussed at length in the FBI's official files on the mutilations in and around Dulce, all of which can be read online on the FBI's website, The Vault (under the title "Animal Mutilation"). So, yes, there is definitely something strange going on in Dulce—something that has been going on for an extraordinarily long time. All of which now brings us to the most controversial aspect of this story—that the Dulce base amounts to nothing less than a vast slaughterhouse. No surprises when it comes to who is being slaughtered. *And why.*

Absorption and Digestion—of Us

If the stories coming out of Dulce really are true, then we may well be in big, big trouble. *All of us*. Rumors suggest that there are multiple levels in the Dulce Base, which is said to extend miles down into the Archuleta Mesa. This is where the ETs are supposedly conducting bizarre experiments and procedures—which involve using us as food items. In *The Dulce Base*, the pseudonymous Jason Bishop III, who also uses the name Tal Lavesque, quoted an insider from the Dulce installation who circulated his own statement to the

UFO community. That man was Thomas E. Castello, who claimed to have worked in the Dulce Base. He said this:

> Level 7 is worse, row after row of thousands of humans and human mixtures in cold storage. Here too are embryo storage vats of humanoids in various stages of development. I frequently encountered humans in cages, usually dazed or drugged, but sometimes they cried and begged for help. We were told they were hopelessly insane, and involved in high risk drug tests to cure insanity. We were told to never try to speak to them at all. At the beginning, we believed that story. Finally, in 1978 a small group of workers discovered the truth.

The alien truth, that is.

Another source who has revealed what he knows about the Dulce Base is Alan B. de Walton, who writes under the name Branton. He claims to know something remarkable—from what was secretly learned by some of the workers who fled for their lives when the aliens gained complete control of the base in 1979—which has a notable bearing on the theme of this book. Branton stated in *The Dulce Book* that during the course of his research he learned that the human body is, in reality, "surrounded by the etheric 'body,' surrounded by the astral 'body,' surrounded by the mental 'body.'"

Now we come to the most important part. One of Branton's Dulce insiders revealed this to him:

We also actually have an extra "body," the emotional "body," that the aliens don't have. This part of us constantly puts out a kind of energy they cannot generate or simulate. This emotional energy ... is, to them, like a potent, much sought-after drug. They can take it out of us and bottle it, so to speak ... Also during this "harvesting," Greys will look directly into our eyes, as if they are drinking something or basking in light.

In a 1991 book, *Matrix II*, Valdamar Valerian refers to one particular alien abductee at the Dulce Base seeing "a vat full of red liquid and body parts of humans and animals ... she could see Greys bobbing up and down, almost swimming."

Joshua Cutchin is the author of a 2015 book, *A Trojan Feast: The Food and Drink Offerings of Aliens, Faeries, and Sasquatch*. Cutchin's findings add to this bleak and harrowing controversy:

> While abduction research does not overtly suggest that aliens are harvesting people for consumption, there may be a grain of truth to the report [contained in the pages of Valerian's *Matrix II*]. "Nourishment is ingested by smearing a soupy mixture of biologicals on the epidermis. Food sources include Bovine cattle and human parts ... distilled into a high protein broth ... "

Faeries, Foyson, and Folklore

David Jacobs is the author of two books on alien abductions, *The Threat* and *Walking Among Us*. He believes that "aliens obtain fuel differently from humans, that their skin has a very unique function, and that they convert 'food' to energy very differently."

This may well be connected to the concept of what is known as "foyson." It's a centuries-old word that is directly linked to another kind of diminutive entity that, just like the black-eyed Greys of ufology, were also renowned for kidnapping people and leading them to magical realms: faeries.

In regards to what foyson is, Patricia Monaghan, in her 2008 book, *The Encyclopedia of Celtic Mythology and Folklore*, explains that "Within every substance on earth is its foyson... the foyson of food is its nourishment, and it was this, Irish folklore contends, that the faeries stripped from food when they stole it. The milk might remain there, creamy in the milk pail, but without its foyson, it had no nourishment left."

This sounds very much like the concept that David Jacobs has suggested—that the aliens convert food into energy in highly alternative ways. It also sounds astonishingly like the stories coming out of Dulce. It's notable that researchers including John Keel and Jacques Vallée postulated that the tales of the Greys of today and the faeries of yesteryear have a common origin. They may well be one and the same—but with identities that have been distorted via cultural beliefs, traditions, and perceptions.

The late US Army Colonel Philip J. Corso, the co-author (with William J. Birnes) of 1997's *The Day After Roswell*, made a very similar observation, too. He speculated that, with regard to the aliens, "if an exchange of nutrients and waste occurred within their systems, that exchange could only have taken place through the creature's skin or the outer protective covering they wore because there were no digestive or waste systems."

All of the above points to the possibility that, when it comes to the extraterrestrials in our midst, their process of ingesting and digesting food is very different from our processes. If all of the above is true, then a vitally important question sorely needs to be addressed: Where are the aliens getting their food supplies? From alien abductees and UFO witnesses, perhaps? An answer to this question comes from the files of Leonard Stringfield, a US Air Force intelligence officer and UFO investigator who died in 1994.

Alien Butchers and the Vietnam War

It was in the late 1980s that Stringfield—still highly active in ufology at the time—received the astonishing and terrible facts concerning an incident that occurred in early 1972, when the Vietnam War was still raging. It took place in Tonlé Sap, Cambodia, which is situated in Southeast Asia. The story is told in Stringfield's *UFO Crash Retrievals: The Inner Sanctum*, which was self-published in July 1991. A group of expert marksmen were secretly and silently parachuted in late one night to an area that bordered closely on North Vietnam. The operation was a vitally important one: to take out a North Vietnamese facility that US intelligence had been able to deduce was clandestinely listening in on top-secret conversations between high-ranking American personnel in South Vietnam. The team camped down for the night, fully prepared to make an assault on the North Vietnamese team as dawn broke. It never happened. Rather, it didn't happen the way that it was envisaged. The group made a skillful and stealthy approach on the area, using the dense foliage for cover, only to find to their terror that something unearthly had changed the situation—and drastically so, too.

As the team got closer to the area in which the North Vietnamese unit was hunkered down, they suddenly found themselves confronted by a large, ball-like craft that sat atop three sturdy, metallic legs. The craft suddenly began to hum—something that caused instant sickness, dizziness, and disorientation on the part of the US troops. Fighting the urge to throw up and get out of the area quickly, they were suddenly rooted to the spot by a group of strange-looking humanoid creatures that today we would call the Greys of UFO lore.

Barely believing what they were seeing, the group was even more horrified by what the creatures were doing: handling various human body parts and placing them into large containers. Arms, legs, torsos, heads—the grisly list went on and on. Some were the remains of white people, others were black. Several looked like Vietnamese people.

Managing to keep the sickness and dizziness under some degree of control, the team crawled forward on their stomachs. The commanding officer silently gave the order to fire; salvos of bullets slammed into bodies of the creatures—who barely seemed fazed by the assault—that is, aside from one, which was said to have been killed by a shot to the head. Several of the US troops lost their lives, and others were left severely burned by the effects of an unknown weapon. The aliens then quickly retreated, loaded the containers into the craft, and vanished into the skies above.

In no time at all, another team was on the scene—"CIA types," as one of the survivors told Stringfield. All of the surviving men were given certain mind-altering drugs to try to make them forget the incredible affair—and apparently they worked. At least, it worked for a while. In the late 1980s, however, two members of the team started to experience dramatic and nightmarish flashbacks to those events of April 1972, which prompted one of the team to contact as many of the others as they could find. Two were dead and three could not be located, but the rest were able to meet up in August 1988 and decided that the story needed telling. After being approached with the story, Stringfield did exactly that: he published it for anyone and everyone that wanted to see it.

This particular incident is not just horrific and disturbing—it also serves to demonstrate how, and under what particular circumstances, alien entities from far away worlds may be using us for nourishment: by effectively slaughtering us and taking our bodies as a means for them to feed, and feed voraciously. Perhaps that is what is going on miles below Dulce, New Mexico.

If you think that all of this sounds way too far out, then consider this: data from the National Crime Information Center's "Missing Person and Unidentified Person Statistics" for 2017 shows that more than 650,000 people are presently unaccounted for—and that's in the United States alone, never mind across the rest of the planet. Of course, many are likely to be child runaways, victims of abusive relationships, criminals, and more. That said, though, there may be more than a few whose disappearances cannot be explained away quite so easily. They may have met their ends deep below the ground... in northern New Mexico.

11
CREATURES THAT MAKE US SICK

It's a fact that when our bodies become depleted of vital energies and essential vitamins and minerals we fall sick—it's all but inevitable, too. One only has to look at two medical conditions that serve perfectly to make that very point. They are anorexia and anemia. The symptoms and side effects of anorexia—the desire to stay thin at all costs, even if the cost is one's health—are many. They are potentially life-threatening, too. They include liver problems, low blood pressure, exhaustion, fainting, seizures, and, of course, weight loss. As for anemia, which is caused by a lowering of red cells in the blood, the symptoms are equally serious: hemorrhaging, ulcers, severe weakness, cramping in the legs, and shortness of breath. And both anorexia and anemia have one grim thing in common: if left untreated, over time they can lead to death.

Of course, anyone—at any time—can fall sick. And just because someone is involved in the world of the paranormal doesn't mean that every illness is somehow connected. It would be absurd to even suggest such a thing. We are all human and, unfortunately, we all get ill—sometimes with minor issues and on other occasions to an extremely serious degree. Particularly intriguing, though, are those cases in which the condition has come on in the *immediate* aftermath of a paranormal encounter; as in hours later—or, at the very most, just a few days.

"Did a Maid Show the Symptoms of Anemia?"

Joseph McCabe, a Franciscan monk who passed away in 1955, knew a great deal about all of this. He spent years poring over ancient texts and doing his utmost to understand the nature of the creatures that so terrified those who lived in Mesopotamia, particularly the Sumerians. McCabe had a particular interest in a pair of highly dangerous demons called Lilu and Lilitu who dwelled in the region. He was clearly aware of how illness was a side effect of a supernatural encounter. He said, in *The Story of Religious Controversy*, "Did a maid show the symptoms of anemia? Obviously Lilu or Lilitu had been busy at night with her body."

McCabe went on to list literally dozens of cases he had on file of people who had nighttime encounters with supernatural entities and who, shortly thereafter, began to exhibit signs of anemia—sometimes acute anemia, but always in incredibly quick time. This all strongly suggests that certain paranormal things were depleting the people McCabe referred to, in significantly dangerous fashion.

A perfect example of someone falling ill very quickly after a paranormal event is that of Albert Bender, the guy who pretty much kicked off the whole Men in Black mystery in the early 1950s. After allegedly getting too close to the truth behind the UFO phenomenon, Bender was visited by three strange and menacing MIB. They were not of the Will Smith and Tommy Lee Jones type, though. Rather, they were far more like today's so-called Shadow People. They were phantom-like things with shining eyes and bad attitudes that walked through the walls of Bender's attic abode in Bridgeport, Connecticut. Bender was terrified by the warnings of the MIB, who told him to quit ufology. Or else.

As it turned out, it took several threats and creepy encounters before Bender finally heeded the words of the terrible trio. When all of this was going down, Bender went down too, with head-splitting migraines, severe stomach pains, faintness, and issues with his short-term memory. And he lost significant weight, suggesting he too was being fed on. Was all of this due to the fear and stress that had been instilled in Bender? Or had he somehow been supernaturally attacked? Who knows? But things didn't end there: Bender—quite out of the blue—developed a fear that he had cancer. Fortunately, he didn't have cancer at all. After quitting ufology and getting married, the symptoms went away and Bender lived to the ripe old age of ninety-four, passing away in 2016.

Dazed, Dizzy, and Meningitis

In early 2016, I spoke with an Englishman, Robbie, who had a disturbing encounter that falls right into this sickness-causing category of paranormal encounters. In August 1982, he had a somewhat similar experience after an encounter with what sounds like one of the Shadow People. Robbie, who was fourteen at the time, was living with his parents in Beckenham, England. He had a traumatic encounter with what he described to me as "a flat black-colored shadow [which] crawled on the bedroom ceiling." During the encounter, Robbie experienced a bout of sleep paralysis and said that the room "suddenly smelled like dirt." Robbie was soon hospitalized with meningitis. It was fortunate that the condition was quickly caught, and Robbie made a full recovery.

There is, however, a disturbing afterword to all this: Several months later Robbie was hospitalized again after fainting while playing soccer at school. He was diagnosed with acute anemia. There is clearly a trend here.

Sugar and Diabetes

In 2015, David Weatherly wrote an article for my *Men in Black* book titled "Children of the Men in Black." The subject was the phenomenon of the Black-Eyed Children. As so often happens when I write a book, people contact me to share their experiences. One of those was Jim, who said that he had an encounter with the BEC in March of 2008, in Florida. At the time, Jim and his wife were living in a rented duplex in a small town outside of Orlando.

Jim's encounter was a typical BEC one: There was a knock on the door late at night and Jim, having peered through the spyhole on the front door, saw two kids in black hoodies, both staring at the ground. He tentatively opened the door and was confronted by a pair of pale-faced, black-eyed monsters—who were now staring right at him. Jim slammed the door and never saw them again. Two days later, though, he experienced a severe case of dizziness, followed by a couple of pretty bad nosebleeds. Then, three weeks later, after feeling repeatedly sick, nauseous, and shaky, he was diagnosed with type 2 diabetes. Jim's blood sugar levels were extremely low. Having read up on the BEC phenomenon, Jim wonders if his diabetes was somehow provoked by BEC so adversely affecting him at the time of his encounter.

Then there is the account of Michelle, a resident of Nova Scotia, Canada. In January 2017, just two days after having a graphic dream about the Slenderman, Michelle was hospitalized with severe ulcerative colitis, which she had never had before and which led her to drop five pounds in just a few days. She finally made a good recovery, but was shaken by the timing of the onset of the condition, which she believed (and still believes) was connected to the skinny monster of her nightmare.

It's important to note that the various conditions discussed in this chapter are anemia, colitis, and weight loss. All three are connected to food and digestion.

And on the matter of weight loss…

Wasting Away

One of the strangest cases in my files comes from a woman who, back in the 1990s, had a series of experiences that left her seriously ill, and took her several months to fully recover from. Alison, of Texas, was seventeen when, in late 1998, she began to feel ill. The first symptom was a rapid loss of weight—around ten pounds in less than a month—which is definitely not a good thing. Given her age at the time, it's perhaps not unreasonable that Alison's mother tactfully asked if all was okay with her. When her mother brought up the issue of her weight loss, Alison became noticeably defensive, but denied that she had anorexia or a somewhat related condition, bulimia.

Nothing more was said. Alison continued to have a healthy appetite, despite steadily losing weight. It was around ten days later, however, that Alison's mother became deeply worried. Early on a Sunday morning Alison screamed for her mother, who quickly came running to her bedroom. To her horror, she saw Alison lying on the bed, her face deathly pale. When her mother tried to help Alison to sit upright, Alison's eyes rolled into her head and she fainted. Luckily, the pair lived only a few minutes from the local hospital, so Alison's mother got her into the car and raced to the emergency room. In no time, she was being examined.

As Alison—who regained consciousness in the car, but still felt weak and dizzy—rested, a doctor asked her mother about Alison's general health. She explained that Alison had lost a lot of weight in the last few weeks. Maybe not surprisingly, the doctor also asked questions about anorexia and bulimia. When Alison recovered, the pair left the hospital, with the doctor suggesting to Alison's mother that she keep a very close eye on her daughter, saying that if she had any more fainting spells to take her to their regular doctor. They were wise words: Alison fell sick on three more occasions, as her weight continued to plummet: a final total of approximately twenty pounds in around six weeks. She was admitted to hospital and watched very carefully.

Tests showed that, physically, Alison was exhibiting all the signs associated with early anorexia. But there was always someone with her when she ate her meals in her hospital room—and at home, too. In fact, she was eating eagerly. On top of that, Alison's mother sat with her for hours after eating each meal—on the suggestion of one of the doctors, to make sure she didn't make herself ill, as is common with bulimia, by vomiting up her meals. Further tests were run but no answers were to be found. At least, not by conventional medicine.

A Chilling Nighttime Visitor

At the height of her illness, when Alison even started to take on a jaundiced look, she confided in her mother that there was something she had not told her—or the doctors.

Alison's mother feared, initially, that her daughter was going to say she had been using and abusing hard drugs. But no. Alison said that four or five days before she began losing weight, she woke in the dead of night to see a pale-faced woman, attired in a long, black, hooded robe, standing next to the bed. The woman was very tall—around six foot three or four. Her skin was white, and her eyes were staring and bulging. Alison found herself unable to move as the woman closed in on her, looming over the bed. The woman gave a loud, satisfied groan at the very same time that Alison suddenly felt ill and cold. The woman retreated into the darkness of the bedroom and vanished.

Alison put the whole thing down as a bad dream—and told her mother that she didn't think any more about it—that is, until the pale hag returned the next night, and the next night, and... well, you get the picture. Alison's mother listened, in fear and dread, as her daughter told her how, every night for weeks, the woman appeared in the bedroom. And all the while, Alison was getting sicker and thinner. Alison even claimed to have seen the woman in her hospital room—as if, said Alison, the Woman in Black knew where she was at all times.

Alison confided one other thing to her mother: four or five nights before the woman first appeared, Alison and two of her friends had been playing with an old Ouija board. Alison's mother was more terrified than she was angry—after all, she only wanted to get her daughter well, not pass judgment when she was severely ill.

Cleansing the Home as Good Health Returns

As luck or fate would have it, Alison's mother had a friend, Jennifer, who worked in the field of alternative medicine and who also had deep knowledge of the world of the supernatural. Jennifer agreed to perform a cleansing of not just the family home, but also of Alison herself. Since the pale, supernatural woman only ever appeared at night, Jennifer said it would be a good idea for her to sit in the bedroom while Alison slept—to ensure that if the woman did appear she would be ready to deal with her.

Jennifer arrived the following evening, armed to the teeth with just about everything she needed to ensure that the evil entity in the home would be banished for good. Jennifer's weapons included sea salt, which is said to have the ability to prevent supernatural creatures from crossing certain thresholds, including doorways to rooms. So Jennifer scattered liberal amounts of sea salt at the front and back doors of the home, in front of Alison's bedroom, and across the windowsill in her room. That was followed by the use of what is known as a *sage smudge stick*. Traditionally, for centuries, sage has been seen as both a powerful protector and a cleanser. So Jennifer did what she does best: she performed a lengthy cleansing program that went on for several hours and involved her lighting the smudge stick and ensuring that the smoke reached all corners of the home. Then, it was a case of watching and waiting.

Alison's mother stayed in the living room at the suggestion of Jennifer, who sat by Alison's bed, ready for just about anything. The black-garbed woman did not put in an appearance, but there were two inexplicable things that did happen that night: Alison's bedroom was briefly filled with an odor like rotting meat and, for a few moments, rapid scratching noises were heard on the walls of the bedroom. Alison and Jennifer held hands tightly and prayed that the hideous thing would leave—and leave now. By all accounts, the rituals worked. The eerie woman was never seen again and over the course of five or six weeks, Alison's health returned to normal. Today, now in her late thirties, Alison is convinced that whatever the woman was, she was feeding on her, which led to the weight loss and anorexia-like side effects and symptoms. To this day, Alison keeps both sea salt and sage in her home in Arizona.

12
BEDROOM INVADERS

Almost certainly connected to the issue of orgone and sexual energy is the issue of supernatural entities that invade bedrooms and engage in what are almost always traumatic experiences of the sexual kind. We've seen how paranormal creatures are attracted to so-called Lovers' Lane locations. There is very little doubt, though, that the most terrifying beings that fall into this bedroom invader category are the succubus and the incubus. In his 2011 book, *Strange Intruders*, David Weatherly says that these creatures "live in a spirit world and crave the energy and life essence of the living."

They are dangerous, violent, and manipulative things that often present themselves in the form of a person's definitive fantasy. There is, however, nothing appealing about these monsters of the night. In fact, they should be avoided at all costs. It's either that or ultimately pay a terrible price.

The problem is that it's very difficult to escape their clutches when you are in bed, completely paralyzed, and held down by a malevolent thing from another plane of existence.

The term "incubus" is a most appropriate one, as it is derived from the ancient Latin term *incubare*, which means "to lie upon." In essence, the term is a most apt one, as the incubus does exactly that: it lies upon its victim and sexually assaults them. The incubus is the male version of this menacing beast, while the succubus is the female. It's a phenomenon that has been with us just about as long as civilization has existed. As evidence of this, we'll now take a trip back to the world and the people of Mesopotamia, which, thousands of years ago, was situated in the eastern part of the Mediterranean, covering Turkey, Iran, Iraq, and Syria.

Beware of the Night Hag

Mesopotamia has a long and rich history attached to it: it was where, around twelve thousand years ago, the Neolithic Revolution began. It was the time period in which we, as a species, went from being wandering hunter-gatherers to people who put down firm roots and began to grow our own food, rather than scavenge to survive. In that sense, Mesopotamia can be seen as a definitive cradle of civilization. And it was in the heart of Mesopotamia that the most dangerous of all the many and varied succubi in history chose to hunt. Her name was Lilith. And *hunt* is a most appropriate term to use, since Lilith would mercilessly pursue and plague her victims until she got what she wanted:

sex, or sexual energy. It should be noted, though, that some religions—such as the Jewish and Pagan faiths—revere Lilith. In that sense, an argument can be made that Lilith has had a bad rap (in the eyes of some, at least).

The name itself, Lilith, is very important. Like the word *incubus*, it has a deep, ancient meaning. It means "night hag," a most appropriate term, to be sure. For the people of Mesopotamia, Lilith was to be avoided at all costs—if possible, of course. Her seductive and manipulative ways, though, ensured that most men were unable to resist her hypnotic charms—which seemed inviting, but in reality, were nothing of the sort. Not even Adam himself—yes, *that* Adam, from the Old Testament—was able to keep away from her, as will soon become apparent. As for her modus operandi, Lilith was said to stealthily access bedrooms in the dead of night— usually between 1:00 a.m. and 3:00 a.m., which is when most supernatural activity still occurs today, never mind millennia ago. She would carefully pull back the sheets of her victim's bed, ensure that the man was on his back, and then sexually assault him—usually while he slept. On occasion, though, a man would wake up—in that previously mentioned state of paralysis. Lilith ensured that the man would ejaculate quickly; there was nothing of a loving or sensual nature to all this. Lilith needed sperm, which she would then use to create her very own children. They were hideous, half-human, half-demonic monsters that some researchers believe are still with us today—in the form of the menacing Black-Eyed Children, which is an admittedly intriguing theory. As for the victims, they would feel weak and tired—which only got worse when Lilith made repeat calls in the early hours and yet again drained them of their orgone.

Spirits and Devils

It's hardly surprising that Lilith had such inextricable ties to Mesopotamia—and specifically to the Babylonians and the Sumerians. Within both cultures, there was a strong belief that demons were quite literally everywhere, manipulating and machinating as they ruthlessly saw fit, in ways that made it clear that the people of the particular era were merely the playthings of the demons who were using, abusing, and terrifying them. Particularly feared by the people were female demons, who were seen as the ones, more than any other, to be avoided at all costs—if one *could* avoid them, of course. Lilith was definitely the chief, when it came to she-devils.

Much of the information and lore we have on Lilith and Mesopotamian succubi comes from a groundbreaking book that was published back in 1903. Its title was *Devils and Evil Spirits of Babylonia*. The author was Reginald C. Thompson. He was an English archaeologist who excavated extensively at numerous ancient sites in the Middle East. It was during the course of his digs that Thompson became friendly with many of the locals—something that ensured that he soon learned of the old legends of the incubus and the succubus, which he also learned were still believed in and accepted into the nineteenth and twentieth centuries. Thompson was fascinated with, but also somewhat disturbed by, the tales of Lilith and her motley band of night monsters. The result? He chose to chronicle the history of the demons of the area in his aforementioned, now-acclaimed book. For many, the book was a wake-up call: the legends of old were more than legends—and the creatures of old were still very much among us.

But what of the connection to Adam? What does the story tell us about Lilith? Let's see.

"I Was Created Only to Cause Sickness"

To understand how, and under what particular circumstances, Adam and Lilith came to be husband and wife, we have to first look at the pages of the Old Testament, and the creation of Adam and Eve. It's a little-known fact that the Bible is in deep conflict when it comes to precisely how the human race came into existence. Certainly, the Holy Bible provides us with the following explanation. In Genesis, Chapter 1, Verses 26–27, we are told,

> Then God said, "Let us make mankind in our image, in our likeness, so that they may rule over the fish in the sea and the birds in the sky, over the livestock and all the wild animals, and over all the creatures that move along the ground.
> So God created mankind in his own image, in the image of God he created them; male and female he created them."

The above quote is taken from Genesis, Chapter 1. If, however, we compare that with the words in Genesis, Chapter 2, we see something intriguing: nothing less than a glaring discrepancy. Chapter 1 makes it clear that in terms of God's work, he created both the male and the female. But that's not what Chapter 2 tells us. It explicitly states that Eve was born out of one of Adam's ribs. There is, without doubt, a conflict here. It can't be both. The conflict was not ignored, however—even though it is seldom touched on in today's Christian teachings.

Jewish lore—specifically that which was developed in the Medieval period—allows for both scenarios to have validity. The Jewish religion offers the theory that yes, God created the human race—men and women, together—but that God, in a unique act, formed Eve in a very different way: out of that aforementioned rib. But how can that be? It has to be one or the other, right? Maybe not. The story goes that although Eve was, in essence, created out of Adam, before she was on the scene Adam had an *earlier* wife who was created by God. That earlier wife came into being the same way as Adam and everyone else: she was created in God's image. And who was that first wife? Lilith, that's who. Of course, even among biblical scholars there is a great deal of debate in relation to the angle of Adam having had two wives.

Lore suggests that the union between Adam and Lilith was a highly fraught one: Adam was of the belief—now considered ridiculous, outdated, and outmoded—that the female had to be subservient to the male. Lilith quite rightly rebelled against such draconian ideas. There was something else she rebelled against, as we'll see now. *The Alphabet of ben Sirach* (also referred to as Ben Sira) is a book that was published centuries ago. The precise date is lost to the fog of time, although most scholars agree that it was penned sometime between 700 and 1000 CE. In part, it states:"While God created Adam, who was alone, He said, 'It is not good for man to be alone.' He also created a woman, from the earth, as He had created Adam himself, and called her Lilith. Adam and Lilith immediately began to fight."

And why did the pair fight? Simple: Lilith objected to always having to have sex in—to use an old and quaint term—the missionary position. *The Alphabet of ben Sirach* continues: She said, "I will not lie below," and he said, "I will not lie beneath you, but only on top. For you are fit only to be in the bottom position, while I am to be the superior one." Lilith responded, "We are equal to each other inasmuch as we were both created from the earth." But they would not listen to one another. When Lilith saw this, she pronounced the Ineffable Name and flew away into the air. Adam stood in prayer before his Creator: "Sovereign of the universe!" he said, "the woman you gave me has run away." At once, the Holy One, blessed be He, sent these three angels to bring her back.

The Alphabet of Ben Sirach expands further and states that God thundered that if Lilith came back of her own personal volition, all would be well again and her actions would be forgotten. If, however, Lilith chose to leave Adam for good—which she did—then she would be cursed to lose one hundred of her children every single day. Forever. When the angels caught up with Lilith, she screamed at them: "I was created only to cause sickness to infants. If the infant is male, I have dominion over him for eight days after his birth, and if female, for twenty days."

The Alphabet of Ben Sirach explains further, When the angels heard Lilith's words, they insisted she go back. But she swore to them by the name of the living and eternal God:

> Whenever I see you or your names or your forms in an amulet, I will have no power over that infant.

She also agreed to have one hundred of her children die every day. Accordingly, every day one hundred demons perish, and for the same reason, we write the angels names on the amulets of young children. When Lilith sees their names, she remembers her oath, and the child recovers.

"She Will Become a Haunt for Jackals"

That the ancient she-demons of Mesopotamia would exclusively straddle their male victims suggests that this imagery was passed down through generations and originated with the story of Lilith. She was herself seen in Mesopotamian lore as something demonic to be avoided at all costs; someone who, during sex, preferred to be on top. Certainly, there are many ancient references to Lilith. Isaiah 34: 12–17, in the Bible, says this of Lilith:

Her nobles will have nothing there to be called a kingdom, all her princes will vanish away. Thorns will overrun her citadels, nettles and brambles her strongholds. She will become a haunt for jackals, a home for owls. Desert creatures will meet with hyenas, and wild goats will bleat to each other; there the night creatures will also lie down and find for themselves places of rest. The owl will nest there and lay eggs, she will hatch them, and care for her young under the shadow of her wings; there also the falcons will gather, each with its mate. Look in the scroll of the Lord and read: None of these will be missing, not one will lack her mate. For it is his mouth that has given the order, and his Spirit will gather them together. He allots their portions; his hand distributes them by measure. They will possess it forever and dwell there from generation to generation.

Clearly, Lilith was no normal human woman: she had demonic powers, and she held dominion over newborn babies. Because Lilith, as a result of the word of God, was forced to keep on creating new babies for herself—due to the fact that one hundred were destined to die every single day—she had to find a proactive way to ensure her beloved demonic babies would survive. This brings us to the legend and actions of the succubus.

The only option available to Lilith was for her to supernaturally and endlessly manifest in the bedrooms of sleeping men and assault them, sperm being the vital desire. In some versions of the story, Lilith would get pregnant in the conventional, tried and tested way that women have always gotten pregnant. On other occasions, however, she would masturbate men and collect their sperm. Or, if a man had been masturbating in bed, she would collect that too. She would also drain them of sexual energy—almost certainly Wilhelm Reich's orgone.

Whatever the truth of the matter, the legend of the succubus was born—largely out of the story of Lilith, which dates back to the creation of human life on planet earth. Now we'll see how exactly all of this led to the coming of both the succubus and the incubus, which are still among us today, a true testament to their—ahem—staying power.

The Development of the Incubus and the Succubus

St. Augustine, a noted philosopher and Christian theologian who was born in 354 and died in 430, commented on this issue. In a post called "Whether the angels have bodies naturally united to them?" the words of St. Augustine are quoted: "Many persons affirm that they have had the experience, or have heard from such as have experienced it, that the Satyrs and Fauns, whom the common folk call incubi, have often presented themselves before women, and have sought and procured intercourse with them. Hence it is folly to deny it."

As this particular extract demonstrates, the term "incubi" was around millennia ago, as was the connection between the incubi and sex. Such things were also being talked about more than a thousand years later.

Malleus Maleficarum is a book that was written in the latter part of the fifteenth century by Heinrich Kramer. Kramer, a priest, said,

> At first it may truly seem that it is not in accordance with the Catholic Faith to maintain that children can be begotten by devils, that is to say, by Incubi and Succubi: for God Himself, before sin came into the world, instituted human procreation, since He created woman from the rib of man to be a helpmeet unto man. But it may be argued that devils take their part in this generation not as the essential cause, but as a secondary and artificial cause, since they busy themselves by interfering with the process of normal copulation and conception, by obtaining human semen, and themselves transferring it.

Kramer added,

> Moreover, to beget a child is the act of a living body, but devils cannot bestow life upon the bodies which they assume; because life formally only proceeds from the soul, and the act of generation is the act of

the physical organs which have bodily life. Therefore bodies which are assumed in this way cannot either beget or bear. Yet it may be said that these devils assume a body not in order that they may bestow life upon it, but that they may by the means of this body preserve human semen, and pass the semen on to another body.

Moving on to more modern times, Paul Carus penned *The History of the Devil and the Idea of Evil* in 1900. He offered his readers the following words:

> Satan is supposed to serve first as a succubus (or female devil) to men, and then as an incubus (or male devil) to women; and St. Thomas declares that children begotten in this way ought to be regarded as the children of the men whom Satan served as succubus. They would, however, be more cunning than normal children on account of the demoniacal influence to which they were exposed in their pre-natal condition.

Matthæus Paris mentions that within six months one such incubus-baby developed all its teeth and attained the size of a boy of seven years, while his mother became consumptive and died.

Bedroom Invaders in Today's World

It's important to note that such creatures are not limited to just one or two parts of the planet—or even to specific time frames.

Incubi and succubi are everywhere—exactly as they were in the distant past. In Newfoundland, there is the Old Hag, a female monster that, just like Lilith, straddles the unwary in the dead of night and steals semen from terrified men. South Africa has the monstrous Tokoloshe. Scandinavia is home to the Mare, which, rather notably, is where the word "nightmare" comes from. Popobawa creates fear and dread for the people of Zanzibar. The Karabasan is a Turkish version. And the Lidérc plagues the people of Hungary. While the names are many and varied (the list above is just the beginning), the key component of a sexual encounter in the dead of night in which the victim is unable to stop the experience is worldwide.

Is it possible that all of this, from the earliest years of civilization—around twelve thousand years ago—to the present day, is due to nothing stranger than the complexities of the human mind? After all, twelve thousand years may be a long time, but we really haven't changed that much. Admittedly, yes, technologically speaking, we are very different from the people of yesteryear. On the other hand, though, just like today, the people back then had families and friends, they laughed and they cried. In that sense, our minds are not so different. Those who are skeptical of the idea that bedroom invaders of a supernatural nature really exist suggest that all of the above—from the distant past to the present day—can be explained away by what is known popularly as *sleep paralysis*. Its medical term is *hypnagogia*—it's a period during the sleep state when a person semiawakens. And in that half-awake, half-asleep state, the brain can do some very strange things, including creating a sense of something threatening in the bedroom. It's a condition which was discovered back in the 1800s by Louis Ferdinand Alfred Maury, who was a French doctor.

Sleep paralysis does not—and cannot—explain away everything, though. There are, for example, cases in which the encounter leaves behind residual odors, such as brimstone and sulfur—which are reported in numerous paranormal encounters. This includes the early 1950s-era experiences of Albert Bender, who quickly found himself on the wrong side of the Men in Black when he started to dig into the UFO mystery. On occasion, a wife has seen her husband straddled by one of these crazed things—and vice-versa. As this shows, these encounters are most assuredly not totally internal to the victims: there is an undeniable external aspect, too.

So, this brings us to the most important question of all: What is it that has tormented and tortured so many for centuries, and why?

Back to the World of Orgone

The incubus can take on numerous forms, including those of a handsome man, a reptilian-type creature, and a beast resembling a werewolf—among many others. The succubus typically appears as a beautiful girl or as a wizened old crone. But there are important factors that must not go amiss. Yes, these things can alter their forms. But they are also able to materialize, dematerialize, and—according to some witnesses—walk through walls and doors. In some cases, they vanish in a flash of light. This strongly suggests they are not flesh and blood entities at all, but energy-based beings, just like the djinn of Middle Eastern history. And in the same way that the djinn can feed on the human life force, so the incubus and the succubus almost certainly do too.

In the old legends, these malevolent things would have sex with their victims with the specific intent of creating offspring—particularly the Lilith-type creatures. Yet, an energy-based life-form is certainly not going to procreate and give birth as we do. Semen would be useless to them. In light of this, the most likely scenario is that the old legends were distortions of something else. Perhaps even distortions brought about by the monsters themselves, as a means to mask their true agenda. So what is the answer?

These creatures of the night deliberately place us into extreme states of sexual emotion—which results in an increase of our sexual energies and our libidos. Then, when we are highly sexed, they quickly feed on that mysterious sexual energy that Wilhelm Reich spent so much time investigating in the 1950s: orgone. And when they are finally done with us, they vanish into the night, leaving behind them an endless number of people whose only memories are of a sexual, supernatural assault.

Yet again, we find in our very midst monsters for whom we are fuel.

13
MONSTERS OF A MYSTERIOUS ISLAND

Of the many and varied strange creatures that fall into the domain of cryptozoology, there are few more infamous than the Chupacabra of Puerto Rico. The phenomenon began in 1995, specifically in August. That was when a woman named Madelyne Tolentino reported seeing a truly bizarre-looking beast roaming around Canovanas, which is located in the northeast portion of Puerto Rico. Terrified by the encounter, Tolentino said that the monster briefly in her midst was approximately three feet tall, had large, dark eyes, and a row of, well, *something* running down its head and back. And it ran in an odd, hopping style—not unlike that of a kangaroo. In the immediate days afterward, further sightings of the beast were reported—and in other parts of the island too. Whatever the creature was, it was definitely on the move. Others confirmed seeing the odd protrusions on the head and back of the beast: it was a row of sharp, imposing spikes. One witness who got a little too close to the creature, also in Canovanas, was treated to a view of the creature's huge, dangerous-looking fangs.

In no time at all, the Chupacabra—which is a Spanish term for "goat-sucker," and a name it got because of the fact that the creature is said to predominantly attack goats and suck their blood—became the subject of major discussion in Puerto Rico. It didn't take long before the story reached the rest of the world. Monster hunters and UFO seekers descended on the island in droves, all keen to solve the riddle of what was roaming Puerto Rico—specifically in Canovanas and the heart of the huge El Yunque rainforest.

Since 1995, literally hundreds of reports have surfaced of the creature and its predations on Puerto Rico. In some cases, witnesses described seeing entire packs of the animals hunting in the heavily wooded portions of the island—seeking out goats, pigs, and chickens to satisfy their appetites. Others report having seen the animals entering and exiting some of the many cave systems that pepper Puerto Rico, which has led to the intriguing theory that the creatures are predominantly nocturnal. They surface at night to hunt and feast, and then, as dawn breaks, they return to their dark, shadowy abodes—those very same caves, of course. Given the fact that most of the sightings of the Chupacabra do occur at night, it's highly likely that this theory has more than a bit of merit attached to it. But what exactly *is* the Chupacabra? The theories are many: extraterrestrial creatures, giant bats, monkeys that have been genetically mutated in secret government labs, and surviving relics from the Jurassic era. There is, however, a highly alternative theory for the true nature of the Chupacabra—and it's a theory that ties in with the theme of this book, as you will now see.

A Bloody Nightmare

I have been on many expeditions to Puerto Rico—all to seek out the truth behind the Chupacabra phenomenon. My first trip to the island was in 2004, and the most recent was in 2016. During my visits, which collectively amount to several months in total, I have spoken to many witnesses of the creature and its attacks. As a result, there is no doubt in my mind that the Chupacabra phenomenon is all too real. During the course of my many expeditions, however, I have uncovered something that has largely been overlooked—or deliberately ignored—by others who have sought to solve the mystery of the monster and its origins.

I have found that there is a tendency among the Chupacabra-seeking community to believe that the creatures are flesh and blood animals—of an unknown type—and nothing more. There is, however, a large body of data that suggests the creatures have supernatural origins—an area that many are reluctant to address—and that the one thing they crave more than any other is blood. *Ours.*

It's an intriguing and often overlooked fact that in nearly all of the cases on record, when the Chupacabra attacks, it seldom feasts on the corpses of the animals it slaughters. Rather, witnesses claim, it drains massive amounts of blood from the bodies of the animals unfortunate enough to have been killed. Of course, for some researchers, this is good evidence that the Chupacabras might really be giant vampire bats—which don't actually suck blood, but lap it up after making small cuts on the skin of the animals they feed on. The available data, however, strongly suggests we should look deeper into the supernatural aspects of the Puerto Rican beast.

An Investigation Begins

As I said, my very first trip to Puerto Rico was in 2004, with a team from the Syfy channel's *Proof Positive* show. Along with me was a friend and fellow monster hunter from the UK, Jonathan Downes. For a week or so, Jon and I roamed around the island, tracking down witnesses and securing intriguing stories, all on the Chupacabra. Yes, we obtained more than a few reports of the attacks of the mysterious animals. But we uncovered something else, too. There were fears and suspicions on the part of the locals that the attacks were the work of monsters that dwelled in other—almost magical—dimensional realms and only entered our reality when they needed to feed, or when we invoked them.

That was not all: according to several of the people Jon and I spoke to—which included veterinarians, ranchers, and police officers—there were suspicions that the Chupacabras had been supernaturally summoned. In this scenario, the creatures had been given access to our world by a powerful secret society on the island, one which performed magical rites and rituals to achieve their goals of power and influence. In that secret society, blood was not just part of their rituals—it was seen as something that would appease the bloodlust of the Chupacabra. And here is where things get really controversial.

As I noted earlier in this particular chapter, the animals most often attacked and killed by the Chupacabra are goats, chickens, and pigs. There are, however, more than a few rumors of attacks on people—attacks that Puerto Rican authorities were determined to keep hidden firmly under wraps, which is perhaps understandable. They were said to be attacks that always ended in a violent death for the person in question. If true, it's certainly no surprise that officialdom would do its very best to bury such events, for fear of mass hysteria breaking out.

A Sinister Series of Rituals

One of the most macabre stories told to us on the 2004 trek around Puerto Rico with the Syfy channel came from a woman who lived in Ponce, and whose story is one of the most controversial on record. Julia, as I'll call her, claimed to know a great deal about the secret society that was at the heart of this controversy. There was a very good reason why Julia was so well-informed: her ex-husband was a member of the group. He was also a powerful figure on the island, specifically in the real estate business. He had been invited into the group in 1999, which was around a year before he and Julia married. In fact, it was his connections to the group that led to their divorce less than a year after they married. When Julia's husband finally confided in her the details of his secret life, Julia was outraged—not just because he had kept his other life from her, but also because of what, exactly, he was involved in.

Julia's husband told her that it was due to certain supernatural pacts between the group and the paranormal denizens of realms beyond ours that he now had so much prestige, power, and money. There was, however, a price to pay—as there always is when one makes a deal with malignant supernatural things from other dimensional planes. That price revolved around nothing less than human blood. Julia sat and listened—both horrified and terrified by what she was hearing—as her husband outlined what was going on. It was no coincidence, he said, that his life had massively altered for the better in 1999. It was all down to that invitation and his willingness to do whatever needed to be done to ensure wealth and influence.

Julia's husband had been present at a particular ritual that was held at the spacious home of a Puerto Rican drug baron, who *also* put his "success" down to that same secret society. The story got even more controversial. Julia admitted that she couldn't prove any of what she was telling us back in 2004, but she claimed to have been told of three people on the island who had been paid—and paid very well—to provide the group with supplies of their very own blood, and to discuss it with no one. So the tale went that the people were taken to the location of the meeting, which was high in the hills of the El Yunque rainforest, and the blood was taken by a local doctor, who was also well paid for his actions and his silence.

The three—two women and one man—were one by one placed on a large, ornate altar at which the blood was removed. Then, with the doctor and the three "donors" driven back to their respective homes (after being warned to never, ever discuss what had happened with anyone), the blood was used in a complex ritual to conjure up and manifest a Chupacabra. Julia claimed that her husband assured her that the ritual worked all too well: the group of several dozen—all dressed in cloaks, no less—focused their minds on having the Chupacabra appear before them, which is exactly what is said to have happened.

A Chupacabra Materializes

It was a hellish situation: The lights in the building flickered and the room was filled with a nauseating odor of sulfur. In seconds, the air shimmered—like a heat haze on the road on a hot summer's day—and the creature slowly came into being, hunched over and staring at the group malevolently. Even long-term members of the group were shocked to their collective core by what they were seeing. It was exactly what the group was counting on, but actually seeing the monster up close and personal was something else entirely.

One and all were quietly told to remain as calm as possible, despite the fraught and fantastic nature of the events. There was one thing that none of the members of the group could avoid seeing: the Chupacabra was semitransparent. It was far more spectral than it was physical. That is, until the monster placed its clawed paws into a large bowl, in which substantial amounts of blood had been poured.

Within seconds of the creature doing so, its transparency was no more and it was suddenly a completely physical entity. Julia's husband was unable to explain the process—mainly because no one seemed to understand the full scope of what it was they were dealing with. He did, however, state that the magical nature of human blood—when ingested in large amounts—not only fed the Chupacabra, but also gave it physical substance in our world, in marked difference to the ethereal form it had in its own realm. When the creature was apparently sated and fed, it vanished in a bright blue flash that affected the eyes of one and all present for several minutes.

Julia listened further as she was told that several other such rituals had taken place in the 1990s—the first of which had allegedly led to the beginning of the Chupacabra phenomenon in 1995. Julia sat back, appalled and frightened by what she had heard, not knowing whether to believe it or not. It was, however, the undeniable fear in her husband's eyes that finally convinced her he was telling the truth—a truth that revolved around how the Chupacabra needs to feast on our blood to maintain a foothold in our world. No wonder Julia chose to leave her marriage behind her.

The FBI and a Monster

On my third expedition to Puerto Rico, just a few years later, I heard a somewhat similar story. Yes, there were differences, but the basic plot—the connection between the Chupacabra and human blood—was the same. The source was a rancher who had a controversial story to tell, one that involved none other than the FBI, which has an office in the city of San Juan, the capital of Puerto Rico. This was actually not the first time I had heard of an FBI connection to Chupacabra. In September 2005—which was when I traveled to Puerto Rico for the second time, with a team from Canada's Red Star Films—our guide was a local man named Orlando Pla. He told me that a couple of years earlier the local FBI office had opened a file on the Chupacabra. It was not a file on the beast itself, though. Rather, as Pla told me, the FBI was investigating the theory that the attacks on farm animals were not the work of the Chupacabra, but of occultists who were using the Chupacabra phenomenon as a cover for their own clandestine activities of the sacrificial variety. In some respects, this sounds *very* much like the same group that Julia told Jon Downes and I about back in 2004.

Jorge was the rancher who revealed what he knew of all this. He was someone who I first met with back in 2004, but who didn't want to speak out in front of the cameras and have his identity blown wide open. And who could blame him for that? Jorge was, however, fine about his first name and his hometown being used—but that was about all. Clearly, he had concerns about his safety—which I could tell was the case. Those concerns were more than understandable.

Jorge, like Julia, had heard of a "secret cult," as he worded it, which had strands and tentacles all across the island, specifically in the domain of big business—which *also* echoes the words of Julia. Jorge's animals had been attacked by what was assumed to have been a Chupacabra, and he wasted no time in calling the police. Oddly, though, it was a pair of agents from the FBI—rather than Puerto Rico's local authorities—who responded and turned up to investigate. Jorge, confused by the fact that the FBI would be interested in the killing of five of his farm animals, asked what was going on. He was quietly told that there were suspicions—which mirrored the story told to me in 2005 by Orlando Pla—that the attacks may have been the work of "cultists." The pair had a look around Jorge's property, took a few photos, thanked him, and then went on their way. That was not the end of the matter though.

Several days later, an elderly man dressed in an expensive suit arrived at Jorge's home and practically invited himself in, such was his insistence that he talk with Jorge. It turned out that, somehow, the group that the FBI suspected was using the Chupacabra issue as a cover had learned about the visit by two bureau agents to Jorge's home. The old man—who Jorge said looked pale and sickly—warned Jorge of the perils of even *thinking* about speaking with the FBI again. Although, for someone who seemingly wanted to keep everything under wraps, the old man was oddly talkative, informing Jorge that human blood was at the heart of the Chupacabra manifestations. And that, as Jorge worded it, "blood sacrifice" was integral to the success of "the program."

It must be noted that Jorge's use of the word "sacrifice" was a very controversial one, since it suggested that perhaps some of the people used in these rituals did not just offer a safe amount of their blood, but lost their very lives in the name of the Chupacabra. Try as I might, Jorge would not expand on this matter and I did not learn anything else that might have suggested a line had been crossed to a terrible, unforgivable degree.

Yes, Jorge was told, the Chupacabra was all too real, but the deadly beast could not exist in our world without human blood. The Chupacabra did not live on human blood as a vampire bat might. Rather, it needed "blood energy." With that all said, the old, withered man left and was driven away in a large, black car. Jorge had one more attack on his property four months later—he chose not to report it to anyone except for me, when we finally caught up again.

14
BIGFOOT

When it comes to the matter of Bigfoot, one of the world's most famous monsters, there's no doubt that most people view them as a North American equivalent to the likes of an African gorilla or an orangutan. Certainly, there is no doubt that most cryptozoologists—monster hunters, in other words—view the creatures from that perspective. Many of those who have carefully studied the history of Bigfoot lore suggest that the creatures may represent relic populations of a massive ape that lived in China, India, and Tibet up until around two hundred thousand years ago, when it's generally accepted that the massive apes became extinct. Their official title is *Gigantopithecus blacki*. In terms of what is known about *Gigantopithecus*, we have to travel back in time to a relatively recent period: the 1930s. The immense beast has the thorny problem of nothing less than male impotence to thank for its discovery. For years, Chinese herbalists and doctors have utilized fossilized teeth to create cocktails that they claim can cure the embarrassing ailment of being unable to "get it up." Since the Chinese landscape is rich in fossilized bones, people have made significant profits from selling such items to apothecaries all across China.

It turns out that in 1936 a German man named Gustav Heinrich Ralph von Koenigswald came across a huge fossilized tooth—specifically, a molar—in a Hong Kong apothecary. It was highly fortuitous that Koenigswald was the man that made the discovery, since he was a paleontologist, and instantly recognized the significance of what had fallen into his lap. Not only was the molar a giant size, but Koenigswald was able to determine it came from a primate—and a large one; a very large one. In the immediate years that followed, Koenigswald found further such examples and coined the term *Gigantopithecus blacki*—the first word standing for "gigantic ape" and the latter a reference to a deceased friend, Davidson Black. Koenigswald was temporarily and disastrously interrupted at the height of the Second World War when he became a prisoner of war of the Japanese. Nevertheless, he was not deterred, and when the hostilities were over he continued his quest to understand the true nature and life of *Gigantopithecus*. As did several other people. One of them was an anatomist named Franz Weidenreich.

In his 1946 book, *Apes, Giants, and Man*, Weidenreich made the controversial assertion that Gigantopithecus may have been far more human-like than ape-like. Chinese scientists also got hot on the trail of Gigantopithecus during this same time frame. Then, in 1956, a massive jawbone of the huge ape was unearthed at a cave in Liucheng, China. The result was that, in a relatively short time, a great deal was learned about this previously unheard-of hairy giant. Perhaps most amazing and impressive of all were Gigantopithecus's statistics: estimates suggested that the height for an adult male would have been around ten feet, while it might have tipped the scales in excess of one thousand pounds in weight. As for when it lived, the estimates were intriguing.

One could make an extremely valid argument that since people are still claiming to see giant apes in the very areas where we know Gigantopithecus roamed—such as Tibet, Vietnam, China, and India—this is evidence that the mighty, hairy giant is still among us, but now known by its far more famous name of Bigfoot. There is, however, one problem: due to its massive size, there is a general consensus among primatologists that Gigantopithecus walked on its knuckles, but Bigfoot is almost exclusively described as walking upright, as we do.

The Supernatural Side of Sasquatch

Although most researchers of the Bigfoot phenomenon perceive the creatures to be nothing stranger than either surviving pockets of Gigantopithecus or an ape of unknown classification, the fact is that there is something very strange about

Bigfoot. We might well say *beyond* strange. There are reports of the creatures being completely impervious to bullets. Numerous reports exist of hunters having a Bigfoot in their sights, but the bullets are always seemingly unable to harm the animals—and certainly never, ever kill one. More controversial, there are reports of the Bigfoot creatures vanishing in a flash of light when seen by startled witnesses. In other cases, the creatures just wink out of existence. No one needs telling that this is hardly the behavior of regular animals—known or unknown.

There is also evidence that Bigfoot is a beast that has some pretty extraordinary skills—we might even call them paranormal powers. One of them is to get into the minds of the shocked eyewitnesses. People have told of seeing Bigfoot up close and personal, only to suddenly have their minds swamped with the booming voice of a Bigfoot, warning them to stay away: we're talking about the likes of telepathic communication and extrasensory perception, or ESP, as it's commonly known. Then there is the issue of what is known as *infrasound*—something that more and more researchers believe is directly tied to the Bigfoot phenomenon.

Infrasound is an extremely low frequency sound which, when directly targeted at a person, can cause all manner of distressing feelings and side effects. Today, the US military is actively researching what is known as "acoustic weaponry." By all accounts, hitting an individual with low frequency sound can cause a person's blood pressure to drop to dangerous levels. Their heart rhythm can go out of sync, sometimes to a dangerous degree. Sudden outbreaks of severe anxiety are commonplace, as are nausea, dizziness, light-headedness, and even temporary short-term memory loss. So, you may well ask, what does all of this have to do with Bigfoot?

In many cases, and according to eyewitnesses of Bigfoot, when they were in close proximity to the creatures—and usually when randomly coming across one or more in the woods—they exhibited the very symptoms that directed, low frequency sounds can provoke. The idea that Bigfoot might be able to target us with infrasound is not at all impossible: after all, both giraffes and whales use it for communication. So for Bigfoot to be able to use infrasound—though admittedly in a hostile way, rather than as a means to communicate—is not so strange, after all.

But now we come to what *is* quite possibly the strangest aspects of this controversy: those reports where people claim to have seen Bigfoot not just dematerialize, but quite literally walk through walls. If such accounts are true—and, certainly, there are more than a few such reports on record—then Bigfoot may be that rarest of all the supernatural parasites in our midst: one that has the ability to exist in both physical and ethereal forms.

All of this brings us to the matter of how, just like so many other paranormal entities referred to in this book, Bigfoot sees us as its prey. On the food chain, we're not the top dogs, after all.

A President, a Monster, and a Violent Death

In his 1890 book, *The Wilderness Hunter*, President Theodore Roosevelt described the killing of a woodsman—in either Wyoming or Montana, the president wasn't sure—a couple of decades earlier. It was a story that came to Roosevelt—who was a keen outdoorsman and hunter—by one of the primary players in the saga, a man named Bauman. According to the tale he told the president, Bauman and a friend were deep in the woods, stalking an unknown animal—but one whose tracks clearly showed it walked upright on two limbs, and which was most definitely not a bear. The creature, then, was certainly no normal one. *Ab*normal would be a much better description. And whatever made the tracks certainly wasn't human either: the sheer size of the prints made that very clear.

For days, the two friends trailed the beast that they suspected at the time was stealthily tracking them, too. The story had a terrible ending: Bauman's comrade was violently killed by the beast while Bauman was briefly away from the camp. On his return, Bauman was shocked to see the camp in complete disarray. Shock turned to terror, though, when Bauman stumbled on the body of his friend: the man's neck had been savagely broken and it looked like something large and heavy had trampled the body in crazed fashion, over and over again. Bauman fled the area, not stopping until he finally made it back to civilization. It was a shocking experience, one which Bauman never forgot—indeed, from a psychological perspective it forever scarred him, particularly on future treks into the deep woods of the United States. What became of the corpse of Bauman's friend, no one knows. Dinner, maybe?

A Hideous Beast Beckons

True North: A Journey into Unexplored Wilderness is the title of a 1933 memoir written by Elliott Merrick, who died at the age of ninety-one in Asheville, North Carolina, in 1997. *True North* was Merrick's very first book; his others included *Green Mountain Farm*, *Cruising at Last*, and *From This Hill Look Down*. In *True North*, Merrick told a story of a girl who had a distinctly disturbing close encounter with a Bigfoot that just might have seen her as a tasty meal. The location of what almost turned into a horrific tragedy was Labrador, Canada. The time: roughly twenty years before the book came out, which would have placed the encounter around 1912 to 1914.

Merrick wrote in his book:

> Ghost stories are very real in this land of scattered lonely homes and primitive fears. The Traverspine "gorilla" is one of the creepiest. About twenty years ago one of the little girls was playing in an open grassy clearing one autumn afternoon when she saw come out of the woods a huge hairy thing with low-hanging arms. It was about seven feet tall when it stood erect, but sometimes it dropped to all fours. Across the top of its head was a white mane.

The girl, unsurprisingly, was rooted to the spot with fear. That fear reached fever pitch levels when the half-animal, half-human thing motioned to the little girl—in a fashion that led her to think the beast was calling to her to come closer. If the girl had any plans to do so, they were quickly dismissed when the face of the monster broke out into that of an evil, sinister grin. It was at that point the girl could see the creature's mouth—which was filled with huge, fierce-looking teeth. They were teeth that could easily have ended the life of the girl and made a meal of her. Luckily, the girl was able to summon up the willpower and strength to make a run for it—which she did, back to the home where she lived with her parents. In almost hysterical fashion, the girl blurted out what had happened—something that led her father to hastily and carefully check out the area in question. The animal, however, was already gone. But there *was* some evidence to show that the girl had not simply fallen asleep and had a bad nightmare, or had mistaken a bear for a monster.

Of the evidence, Merrick told his readers,

> Its tracks were everywhere in the mud and sand, and later in the snow. They measured the tracks and cut out paper patterns of them which they still keep. It is a strange-looking foot, about twelve inches long, narrow at the heel, and forking at the front into two broad, round-ended toes. Sometimes its print was so deep it looked to weigh five hundred pounds. At other times the beast's mark looked no deeper than a man's track.

The local folk didn't waste any time at all trying to find the hair-covered beast in their very midst. A posse was soon on the hunt, carefully scouring the nearby woods, which were seen as the most likely location where the creature would hide out. A nighttime stakeout of nearby Mudd Lake proved to be completely fruitless, as did another search of the lake on the following night. Traps were laid down by anxious townsfolk. Nothing worked: the monster was gone. For a while.

When the story reached Merrick himself, he was determined to try to find out if the account was true or a tall tale like the kind that are so often told around campfires. It didn't take Merrick long to learn that the people of Traverspine took the whole thing very seriously—even though by the time Merrick was onto the story it was already an old one. Having gained their trust, Merrick spoke with more than ten locals who had, at various times over the years, seen the unidentified abomination. It clearly wasn't just a one-off event. No one knew what the thing was—only that it was no normal animal.

Merrick added the following, based on what one of his informants in town told him:

> One afternoon one of the children saw it peeping in the window. She yelled and old Mrs. Michelin grabbed a gun and ran for the door. She just saw the top of its head disappearing into a clump of trees. She fired where she saw the bushes moving and thinks she wounded it. She says too that it had a ruff of white across the top of its head. At night they

used to bar the door with a stout birch beam and all sleep upstairs, taking guns and axes with them.

The Town's Dogs Get Antsy

It wasn't just the people of Traverspine that were concerned, either—their pets were too. Specifically, the local dog population. On a number of occasions, the presence of the dogs near the woods of Mudd Lake provoked the monster to howl and growl in frenzied fashion—something which clearly demonstrated the creature knew the dogs were near and reacted in a fashion designed to keep them well away. It worked: the dogs kept away from the area of all the action.

Interestingly, on one occasion, said Merrick, the hairy horror swung at one of the dogs with what was described as "a club." Fortunately, the dog was not injured—but just the fact that the monster had a club, or perhaps a large branch wrenched off a tree, suggests it was an intelligent animal, one that used not just brute force, but weapons too. And then it was all over. After a few years of occasional mayhem, the monster was gone for good.

Missing People and Monsters in the Woods

Cryptozoologist Loren Coleman notes in his 2003 book, *Bigfoot!*, that in the Bigfoot Bulletin of October 31, 1970, published by California researcher George Haas, there is

> a fantastic letter from an army trainee named Nick E. Campbell at Fort Ord, California. He related that

two Texas National Guard privates, one of them a minister, had told him that at Longview where they lived, there were reports from about 1965 of a giant hairy creature roaming the back country between there and Jefferson, Texas. They said that the creature had reportedly killed a couple of people. Reverend Royal Jacobs had told him that as a teenager he was a member of a posse that hunted the creature and he had seen the body of a person the creature had torn apart.

Then there is the not insignificant matter of all the people who go missing every year… *in the woods*. David Paulides is the brains behind a series of books that fall under the Missing 411 banner. North America Bigfoot Search says of his work, on their website,

Missing 411 is the first comprehensive book about people who have disappeared in the wilds of North America. It's understood that people routinely get lost, some want to disappear but this story is about the unusual. Nobody has ever studied the archives for similarities, traits and geographical clusters of missing people, until now.

It's important to note that Paulides is very much open-minded on the issue of who, or *what*, is responsible for the massive numbers of people who enter the woods and forests of the United States only to never be seen again. It's important to note, though, that members of the Bigfoot-seeking community were quick to sit up and take notice of Paulides's important work when it first surfaced—an unsettling area of research that practically no one else has dug into.

Paulides investigated the summer of 1969 disappearance of a young boy named Dennis Martin, who, very oddly, vanished within sight of his father. The location was Cades Cove in the Great Smoky Mountains National Park, which borders upon North Carolina and Tennessee. It's intriguing to note that soon after the incident occurred, a man named Harold Key heard a wild, animalistic scream coming from somewhere near Rowans Creek. Notably, Key, who was with his family walking on a trail, saw something that he at first thought was a bear. Oddly, though, it had certain human qualities to it, which led Key to describe it as a "dark figured, rough-looking man" partially hidden behind a thicket.

What are we to make of these stories of dangerous Bigfoot, of what may very well be *killer* Bigfoot, and of all the many people who are never seen again after taking a trip into the forests of the United States? Yes, some may fall victim to accidents, to ill health, and even to fatal attacks by the likes of bears and mountain lions. There is, however, a body of evidence that suggests Bigfoot are not beyond kidnapping, killing, and maybe even devouring those who intrude upon their territory. Remember that the next time you head out into one of the wilder, denser US forests. Something large and hairy may be sizing you up ... for food.

15
ZOMBIES

Thanks to television shows like *The Walking Dead* and *Zombie Nation*, and movies like *World War Z*, *Dawn of the Dead*, and *28 Days Later*, the zombie is riding high—at least in the world of fiction. It's a little-known fact, though, that throughout history, accounts can be found of creatures that sound very much like the undead. And just like the less-than-living in *The Walking Dead*, these ancient monsters savagely fed on the human race. In many cultures, they still do.

For the people of the many islands that compose the Philippines, the resident zombie is the Aswang. It also has two alternative monikers: the Tik-Tik and the Sok-Sok. The names are taken from the odd noises the creature makes when it is on the hunt for human flesh. The Aswang has another string to its bow—if that's the appropriate terminology to use. As well as lusting after human flesh, the Aswang is also a monster that thrives on human blood. In that sense, the beast is half zombie and half vampire. And all predator.

Ghouls, Graves, and a Black Dog

The Aswang makes for a grim picture: It is skinny in the extreme, as white as a ghost—which is more than appropriate—and its eyes are pale and bulging. As for its clothes, they are typically torn and ragged and they give off a nauseating stench of rotting meat. And it's an extremely fast runner. No wonder the zombie parallels are so evident. Like just about all zombies, the Aswangs live on the flesh of people. Horrifically, they consider newborn babies to be the most prized meal of all—something which has led pregnant women in the Philippines to ensure that their homes are well protected and in lockdown mode at night. Interestingly, the Aswang, just like the Middle Eastern djinn, can take on the form of a large black dog. A connection, maybe?

Moving on, there is the matter of the ghoul. It's a deadly and predatory creature that has a particular penchant for lurking around graveyards. There is a very good reason for this: Just about all the other paranormal parasites described in this book target the living. The ghoul, however, is a monster that craves the flesh, bones, and blood of recently deceased people. It will dig in crazed fashion when its acute sense of smell alerts it to the fact that there is a fresh (or fresh-ish...) corpse in its midst. The creature will use its hands to dig deep into the ground, throwing dirt here, there, and everywhere until it gets what it seeks, and then feeds savagely on the rotting body of the poor, unfortunate soul it has targeted.

A Winged Monster and the Human Soul

Gambia has its very own cursed thing with zombie-like overtones attached to it. Its resident member of the undead is the Kikiyaon. This diabolical West African terror physically resembles a gargoyle or a harpy, of both Roman and Greek lore. A relatively short humanoid creature with bat-like wings and fiery red eyes, the Kikiyaon is a monster that has a long and horrific history—and for a good reason. In English, the word *Kikiyaon* translates to "soul cannibal."

The Kikiyaon typically dwells in caves, usually ones that are well hidden in the jungle environment. When the sun has set and darkness is upon the landscape, the Kikiyaon will soar into the night sky, seeking out the vulnerable, the weak, and the unwary. When it has found its target, the Kikiyaon will stealthily creep into the home of its victim and softly nip their skin—very often on the neck, which of course inevitably provokes vampire imagery. Now we get to the zombie comparisons.

In no time after the person is bitten, their character changes—and hardly in what we would call a positive way. The person loses their character and their face takes on a blank appearance—not unlike that of the old-school type of zombie most associated with Haitian voodoo traditions. There is another zombie angle to all of this: after a person is bitten by the Kikiyaon, the victim becomes ill, his or her skin starts to smell of decaying flesh, and, finally, they die. But they don't stay that way: the bite of the Kikiyaon ensures that they will soon return to the land of the semi-living and go on a ferocious spree of killing and eating.

An Attack of the Worst Kind Possible

Bringing matters very much up to date, there is the matter of a horrific incident that occurred in May 2012, in Miami, Florida. The specific location was the city's MacArthur Causeway. As fate unfortunately had it, shortly after noon a man named Rudy Eugene got on the causeway and, as he neared the far side, had sudden car problems: his vehicle ground to a halt. He had little choice but to leave it where it stood and walk back the way he had originally come from, in the hopes of finding a local repair shop. In between walking back the way he came and reaching his destination, though, something very weird happened to Eugene. In fact, it was something terrible and practically unbelievable—something that we will never really understand.

The bridge was around three miles in length and since it was a hot day, Eugene chose to take a slow walk from one end to the other—something that was confirmed by security cameras positioned on the bridge. As he reached a ramp, Eugene decided to take the exit—even though he should have continued on farther had he wanted to find a repair shop. As Eugene did so, he came upon a man named Ronald Poppo. Down on his luck and his money, Poppo had no place to call home and was lying spread-eagled on the ground, passed out from the effects of booze.

When Eugene reached Poppo, he charged at his face, tearing out both of Poppo's eyes with his teeth and strangling him to the point of unconsciousness. Eugene was far from being done: he then devoured Poppo's face, from the top of his forehead to the base of his chin. A local police officer was quickly on the scene, but it was all to no avail: the damage was done and was irreversible. If the officer thought he had seen it all, he was wrong: when the officer shouted at Eugene to stop, the only response Eugene made was to slowly turn around and *growl* at the horrified policeman. The officer put a bullet into Eugene. It did no good. Neither did the second. The third? Just the same. And that went for the fourth, too. It was only the fifth bullet that killed Eugene and ended his awful attack on Ronald Poppo, who, after surgeries, survived the ordeal.

When Eugene's body was autopsied, the only thing found in his system was cannabis, but that would hardly have led to such a situation. Rumors soon circulated that Eugene had been briefly possessed by a Wendigo—a predatory, flesh-eating creature that is a staple part of the legends of the Algonquin Native American people. The Wendigo is a terrifying and savage monster that can take over the human mind and force that human to do its dark bidding. On top of that, according to Algonquin mythology and history, after one is possessed by a Wendigo they can then become one, too.

Did something occur on the MacArthur Causeway that briefly turned an otherwise normal man—who was trying to find a way to get his car fixed—into a marauding monster, a creature not unlike that which Rick Grimes and his buddies have to combat on *The Walking Dead*? We may never know. All we can say for sure is that, quite out of the blue, unbridled savagery led one man to do his utmost to eat another.

16
ENERGY SUCKERS

We'll end our examination of the terrible things that see us as their food with the most terrifying and menacing of all the many and varied parasitic monsters in our midst. I am talking about the Men in Black. No, not Hollywood's versions of the MIB: Agents J and K, as portrayed on the big screen by actors Will Smith and Tommy Lee Jones. Tinsel Town did a very good job of creating a trilogy of MIB movies that entertained and excited audiences the world over—and made those same audiences laugh loud and hard, too. But there is nothing to laugh about when it comes to the *real* Men in Black. In the movies, the MIB are in the employ of an agency more powerful and far more secretive than even Edward Snowden's old "friends" at the National Security Agency. But we should not forget that the *Men in Black* movies are fiction. Unfortunately, as is so often the case, the real world often outdoes the domain of fiction—and seldom in a positive fashion.

The so-called "modern era" of UFOs began in the summer of 1947, specifically on June 24. That was the date upon which a pilot named Kenneth Arnold encountered a squadron of strange-looking aircraft flying near Mount Rainier, in Washington State—as the man himself noted in his 1952 book with Ray Palmer, *The Coming of the Saucers*.

As an experienced pilot, Arnold was deeply puzzled that he was unable to identify the things ahead of him. As he got closer, Arnold realized exactly why he was unable to figure out what the objects were: they were not regular airplanes, but futuristic-looking half-moon-shaped vehicles that resembled absolutely nothing in the US arsenal at that time. And that was surely the case for the Russians, too. It was not long before word of Arnold's encounter reached the eyes and ears of the media—in fact, it took less than a day. The terms "flying saucer" and "flying disk" all but immediately became the talk of 1947. Today, the term *UFO* is far more popular than the now largely antiquated flying saucer.

The Coming of the MIB

Although the latter part of the 1940s proved to be a period in which sightings of apparently unearthly craft abounded, it wasn't until the early 1950s that the Men in Black stepped out of the shadows—in force—and set about snaring us, manipulating us, and ultimately *digesting* us. And no, the term "digesting" is not an exaggeration.

Over the years there have been numerous investigators of the Men in Black phenomenon, such as UFO researchers Gray Barker, Jim Keith, and Harold Fulton—all of whom are now long gone. None of them, however, came anywhere close to the success of Albert K. Bender—the man without whom our knowledge of the MIB and their agenda would be sorely lacking, and who created the International Flying Saucer Bureau (IFSB). Born in 1922, Bender served his country during the Second World War in the US Army Air Corps. Post–World War II, Bender lived in Bridgeport, Connecticut, in a somewhat creepy-looking old house that stood at what was the junction of Broad Street and North Frontage Road at the time. Today, the house is no more, the secrets it once held now just memories and stories in books.

Adding to the creepy atmosphere, Bender lived in the attic. Of course! Where else? As a fan of the worlds of sci-fi, fictional horror (H. P. Lovecraft was one of Bender's favorites), and the real world of the paranormal, Bender radically altered his attic room into what he called his "Chamber of Horrors." Paintings of grotesque monsters filled the walls. Imagery of skulls and black cats abounded. A gothic-style painting of an old cemetery dominated the room. And plastic spiders hung from the ceiling. Then there was Bender's altar—and it was at the foot of that unsettling place of worship that Bender would engage in infernal rites designed to provoke a supernatural response from … well … who knows what? Bender didn't care what "it" was, he just wanted that reply. He got it, alright. He opened the kind of door that it's never, ever wise to open. And *something* came through.

Food for Thought—and for the Men in Black

As Albert Bender noted in his 1962 book, *Flying Saucers and the Three Men* (zero prizes for guessing who the "three men" were...), practically no time after he called forth something supernatural from the other side, he was paid a visit. Yes, the Men in Black had picked up on Bender's request for communication—and they responded in kind. Bender was replying to a mountain of mail from the readers of his latest issue of *Space Review* magazine when he received his first visit of what eventually amounted to several.

It was late one night in 1953 when the MIB turned up. There was no slow, loud knock at the door, though. Nor were any US government ID cards flashed. Bender's Men in Black walked *through* the walls and door of the attic. They were blazing-eyed, skinny, pale monsters. Their mode of dress was black suits, black fedoras, skinny black ties, black shoes, and crisp white shirts. Imagine a 1950s-era member of the Mafia mixed in with a liberal amount of a resurrected zombie that has seen better days, and the image swirling around your mind won't be too far off of what Bender encountered.

As the Men in Black got closer, Bender started to feel sick. Nausea overwhelmed him and an odor of sulfur filled the attic. Worse still, Bender felt himself becoming weak. His energy levels plummeted like those of a diabetic who has missed breakfast, lunch, and dinner. He was freezing cold and the shakes had suddenly set in. Even in his hazy, sickly state, Bender couldn't fail to see something that chilled him to the bone: the weaker he got, the brighter and more fiery the eyes of the terrible trio got. Weaker, brighter. Weaker, brighter. You get the picture. Bender certainly did. In a macabre and terrifying way... *Albert Bender was, bit by bit, being eaten—devoured, even.*

With Bender sprawled out on the bed, as helpless as a newborn puppy, the Men in Black telepathically warned him to leave the UFO subject alone. If he didn't, something terrible would befall him. The three turned on their heels (black, of course) and dematerialized as mysteriously as they had first appeared. Bender was no fool: he knew that if he didn't quit chasing flying saucers the MIB were likely to turn his life into a living hell. But the allure of the space beings and their silvery, saucer-shaped craft was way too strong. So, it was all but inevitable that Bender would get another visit. And another. He did. Things got worse and worse: like those ghoulish drivers who can't keep their eyes off of a fatal car accident on the highway, the MIB couldn't keep away from Bender. They would always arrive at night and hover over the bed, as Bender fell into that same state of sudden illness and weakness that hit him on the first occasion.

Bender Quits Ufology

By the second visit, Bender's health was suffering significantly; he had gotten progressively weaker. He started to develop stomach problems. From his descriptions, it may have been ulcers and a dose of ulcerative colitis. His energy levels had fallen off the scale and he lost weight. He was constantly out of breath. Migraines plagued him day and night. As for those MIB? Well, their eyes just proceeded to get brighter and brighter with every visit. It didn't take Bender long to realize that he was effectively being bled dry. It was, in a strange way, very similar to the actions of those black-cloaked vampires who drained bevies of buxom babes of their blood in the likes of Universal's 1931 version of Bram Stoker's classic novel, *Dracula*, starring Bela Lugosi. In a very strange bit of twisted irony, the movie was one of Bender's all-time favorites.

Come the third visit, Bender was not in a good condition at all: he was now seeing the MIB in the darkened streets of town. They would stand on the street corner, leering at him—entities that no one but Bender could see. The stomach problems were getting worse. He was losing more weight. Bender knew he had to do something. And he did. Bender, albeit somewhat reluctantly, walked away from UFOs and closed down *Space Review*. Bender shut the doors on the IFSB, too, and quit the subject. He made a very brief reappearance in 1962, to write the aforementioned *Flying Saucers and the Three Men*, after which he left the subject behind and never returned. From the 1960s until his death in 2016, Bender was, when it came to UFOs, permanently AWOL.

Albert Bender was not only the man who effectively birthed the MIB enigma; he was also the first person to astutely realize that the Men in Black were *feeding* on him. And on who knew how many more people. Bender didn't even want to think about that.

Let's now take a look at an absolute catalog of such cases in which the Men in Black demonstrate an aversion to conventional food and liquid and appear to be using us as a form of fuel.

UFOs, Migraines, and Plummeting Energy Levels

John Keel, the author of the acclaimed 1975 book *The Mothman Prophecies*, was someone who had a deep interest in the Men in Black enigma and who even found himself in their clutches from time to time. Of the many cases that Keel personally investigated, one of the strangest has a significant bearing on the story told in this final chapter. It all occurred in May 1967, even though the affair had its origins in late 1966. It's a story that Keel shared in his 1970 book *Operation Trojan Horse*.

The location was a field in a rural part of the city of Owatonna, Minnesota—which just happens to be the home of the expansive Kaplan's Woods, which are said to be haunted by multiple disembodied spirits of a terrifying nature. But it's UFOs and Men in Black that we are focusing on now, not the restless dead. It was late at night when Mrs. Ralph Butler and a friend were staring at a patch of the night sky, watching a curious display of unidentified bright lights dance around.

Without warning, one of the lights dropped from the heavens at high speed. Just before it hit the ground, the UFO came to a sudden halt, bobbing a few feet above the field floor, not unlike a boat on the ocean. Without warning, Mrs. Butler's friend—who declined to have her name used by Keel—fell to the ground and went into a trance. In what seemed to be akin to a case of demonic possession, the woman began to speak in a deep, almost robotic fashion. "What is your time cycle?" asked the voice. Mrs. Butler, in her own voice, replied, "A day is approximately twelve hours long and a night is twelve hours long." The strange question-and-answer session continued for a few more minutes, after which the woman finally came around. The light shot away, vanishing into the night sky. Ominously, for the next few days, whenever the women tried to share the details of their encounter, they were hit by pummeling migraines and weakness. But there was something else, too.

The MIB Who Didn't Know How to Eat

During the course of the interview between Mrs. Butler and John Keel, something very intriguing surfaced. Quite out of the blue, she asked Keel if he knew anything about mysterious men visiting UFO witnesses, men who looked like military personnel, but who may not have been. Keel, hardly a stranger to the MIB phenomenon, played matters down a bit and said that, yes, he had heard a few such stories. Actually, Keel had dozens of such cases on record, but he didn't want to risk putting words into Mrs. Butler's mouth, or of influencing her. Keel sat back and listened as Mrs. Butler told her story.

It was in May 1967, some six months after the UFO sighting, that a "Major Richard French" turned up on Mrs. Butler's doorstep, identifying himself as a representative of the military and asking questions about flying saucers. Just like all of the Men in Black, there was something just not right about Major French: his skin was an odd shade of olive. His face was extremely pointed, particularly his chin. He spoke English, but his accent was as blank as it could be. And he was dressed in a suit and a black tie, rather than in a military outfit.

Very oddly, Major French—quite out of the blue—said that his stomach was causing him some trouble. Mrs. Butler offered him some Jell-O, which he declined. He quickly left. The next day, though, the major was back. Yet again, he complained about his stomach. Mrs. Butler again offered him a bowl of Jell-O, hoping that it might help the major. Here is where surreal became *beyond* surreal. For a moment or two, Major French stared at the Jell-O, seeming completely unware of what it was. He then stared at the spoon Mrs. Butler had given him as if he had no comprehension of what it was. He awkwardly picked up the bowl and proceeded to try to *drink* the Jell-O. Mrs. Butler went silent and stared in disbelief. Major French did not hang around, realizing, it seems, that Mrs. Butler knew something was not quite normal—which is an understatement of epic proportions. He quickly left, never again bothering Mrs. Butler.

Staring at a Steak, but Not Eating It

Cases abound of Men in Black not understanding what regular food is, and also having no understanding of how to eat it. In roughly the same time frame that Mrs. Butler of Owatonna, Minnesota, had a couple of strange encounters with Major Richard French, another weird "man" walked into Max's Kansas City, a diner in New York, and asked for food. His suit was black and decades out of style, and his eyes bulged, like mad dog eyes. "Something to eat," he said in a monotone, robotic fashion. It was followed by one more word: "Food." Clearly, this particular MIB was a man of very few words. The man, John Keel reported in 1975's *Visitors from Space*, stared menacingly at the waitress, who suggested a steak, while she cautiously backed away. The juicy steak was duly brought to the table but it remained untouched: knives and forks were beyond the comprehension of the man, who—quite out of the blue—claimed to the waitress that he was an extraterrestrial entity. He soon left, evidently not happy with what passes for food on earth.

Curt Sutherly, writing in 2001's *UFO Mysteries*, described another report from 1967. In this case, the location was Colorado's San Luis Valley. The witness was Mrs. B., a skilled artist living in the area. A mysterious man visited the woman, and made this very odd statement to her: "I cannot read, but mention any book in any library and I will be able to tell you its contents." In a very revealing situation—perhaps even a bit *too* revealing—he then told the slightly unsettled artist that the human race spends far too much time on food and energy, when both could be extracted from the atmosphere. The MIB left as enigmatically as he had arrived.

The "Gauzy" MIB

Denise Stoner is a well-respected investigator of the UFO phenomenon who lives in Florida. Along with Kathleen Marden, she penned the book *The Alien Abduction Files*. The pair chronicle numerous cases of high strangeness. On several occasions Stoner has encountered, in the restaurant of her local Whole Foods, a strange and unusual character: a man who wears sunglasses and a panama-style hat. His wispy hair is gauzy too. Of course, some might say that the man in simply another customer. The fact that Stoner has had numerous run-ins with both Men in Black and Women in Black strongly suggests otherwise.

Notably, the man almost obsessively stares at Stoner, *never, ever touching the food or drink that is always in front of him*. It's almost as if they are there simply as decorations, which may indeed be the case. Certainly, they're not items that the creepy character seems to be particularly interested in. There is clearly something very wrong with the strange man who never eats or drinks. Just as Stoner is about to finish her snack, the man appears to know that this is a signal she is about to leave and he stands up. He always makes sure he walks past Stoner's table, rounds a corner and vanishes—quite literally—as he passes a large pillar on the corner of the shopping plaza.

Avoiding Food

Moving across the Atlantic, Neil Arnold, England-based author and researcher of all things supernatural, ufological, and monstrous, had an experience in London in the early 1990s that eerily mirrors that of Denise Stoner years later. Notably, with his writing career still then in its relative infancy, Arnold chose to chronicle the matter of the MIB. His accounts of supernatural activity in the UK's capital city can be found in his 2010 book, *Paranormal London*. It's interesting to note that Arnold's encounter took place only a month or so after he and a couple of friends had a UFO encounter as they walked to their respective homes late at night. In light of that, it's probably not a coincidence that Arnold had his very own confrontation with a particularly hostile MIB, one who absolutely oozed menace.

It was early in the afternoon of one particular day, and with the same two friends, Arnold paid a visit to the McDonald's restaurant in Leicester Square, London. The three mates sat down and started to munch on their food. As they did so, they couldn't help but notice a certain man was watching them—and watching them eerily and with deep hostility, it might be said. Arnold says that the man was around seventy years old, had slicked-back hair and, most unusual of all, as Arnold stared back he saw that the man never blinked. And he did not touch his food. As for his clothing, it was (what else?) a black suit, a white shirt, and a dark-colored tie. Arnold developed a deeply unsettling feeling that the man's penetrating eyes were piercing his very soul—feeding on him, almost. In a very atypical fashion, the three quickly exited the restaurant. They did not look back—which was probably a wise decision.

"Harvesting Something"

Jo Ann Koch has had a number of close encounters with the Men in Black, which give every indication that she has been bled to the bone by these energy sucking entities. Her accounts of encounters with otherworld entities appear in her 2015 book, *Aliens, Abductions and Other Curious Encounters*. She says, "I have been 'visited' since I can remember, as early as age 2/3. I'm now a senior citizen and very few people know of my experiences."

Notably, Koch has come to the conclusion that during the alien abduction experience, the Grey aliens are "not really experimenting on us but are harvesting something." This very much echoes the stories coming out of Dulce, New Mexico.

Of equal note, Koch says this after one particular encounter with the MIB: "I got weaker and weaker and was quickly admitted to the hospital when my hemoglobin went down to 6. I had an emergency transfusion of two pints of blood. I ended up with five-plus doctors and various others who worked on me for eight months."

"Neither Had Taken Even a Single Sip from Their Beers"

The following account, sent to me by a Facebook friend, is without doubt one of the most disturbing and chilling stories I have on record, and I don't make such a statement lightly. The source—who prefers the nickname "A Hesitant Believer"—says this of an experience which occurred in late 2008:

> I worked as a bar manager at a sports bar in Tampa, Florida, and at 2:00 AM I cashed out the servers and sent them home and closed down the kitchen. The bar itself closed at 3:00 AM, but my last few barflies stumbled out before 2:30. I closed out the credit cards, counted the register, abused my free credits on the jukebox, and sat down to wait out the clock. At about ten minutes to three a couple walked in. I told them it was last call and cash only at this point, and locked the doors behind them, not even really paying attention to them (rude, I know, but after 12 hours, give me a break). When I did notice them, I began to feel uneasy.
>
> Neither one of them sat down on the stools in front of the bar. They each ordered a non-alcoholic beer, and then just stood there holding their drinks, about two stools apart. Then I noticed how they were dressed. I dress in a "goth" style and prefer black, but these two were definitely not

goths, despite the (almost) all-black attire. The man, who appeared older than the woman, maybe about 40-ish, wore a black double-breasted suit of an outdated cut. I'd say maybe 1950s style, with a rumpled black shirt and a crooked black tie.

I'd say he was about 5'9" with a thin build. He had incredibly pale skin that showed blue veins underneath (I had turned on all of the house lights by this point, so they stood out in stark contrast), a very high forehead, prominent cheekbones, and deep-set, large, brilliant blue eyes, possibly the most vibrant blue I have ever seen. He had thin, dry, unhealthy-looking, silvery-grey hair pulled back in a ponytail, with seemingly random dark brown patches in it, as if he gave a half-assed attempt to dye it and gave up halfway through the process.

The woman, who was about 5'6", emaciated, and looked about mid-20s, wore a black evening gown with elbow-length satin gloves and had a clashing bright green knit shawl around her shoulders. She had a short bob haircut with bangs, though it really looked like a poorly cared-for wig. She had the same high forehead, cheekbones, and blue eyes as her partner, although her eyes were more narrow and slightly slanted. Neither one had eyebrows.

As they were leaving, the pair gave "AHB" very disturbing grins. *Neither had taken even a single sip from their beers.* And then something disturbing happened: within seventy-two hours, "AHB" says, "I developed a severe bacterial infection on my legs and lower abdomen. It was a Strep infection, and the doctor could not determine how I contracted it."

As all of the above shows, there are three primary angles when it comes to the Men in Black. One: there is the matter of the MIB clearly not being able to eat or drink the kinds of things that we would not think twice about having, such as a tasty steak, a cold bottle of beer, or a bowl of Jell-O. Two: we have the issue of the Men in Black "harvesting" us—as Jo Ann Koch astutely and concisely worded it. And three: let's not forget the very disturbing fact that when the MIB target their victims for food of an energy type, those same victims find themselves plunged into states of severe illness and a weakening of the body to a dangerous and almost fatal degree.

A word of advice: If, late one night, there is a loud knocking at the door and you look through the spyhole to see a trio of pale, ghoulish Men in Black, don't open the door under any circumstances. Just carefully and quietly back away. Doing so may just save your life. And it may prevent you from becoming something's fuel.

CONCLUSION

Now it's time for us to reach some conclusions on the matter of the many kinds of paranormal parasites that invade our world and deliberately seek us out and target us for energy and food. As we have seen, tales of creatures that invade our space and callously bleed us dry are not just many in number; they also extend back into the very earliest years of human history. In other words, for as long as humankind has existed, those supernatural things that exist in realities very different from ours have had the perfect, unending food supply. Us. In light of all this, and taking into consideration the stories of the genetic manipulation of early humans in the distant past, one has to wonder if we were deliberately engineered to be the cattle of someone else. Is the earth just one big farm? If so, who or what is the farmer? Were our fates laid out for us long before we, *Homo sapiens*, even existed? And what is the fate of those who call the farm their home today? These questions are as important as they are disturbing. The answers may be even worse.

If there is one thing that can be said with a high degree of certainty, it's that the vast majority of the human race is woefully unaware of the incredible scale on which the feeding is taking place—and why. It's exactly the same for the cows in the fields who happily munch on their grass—that is, until the time comes when they are dispatched to the slaughterhouse. They, just like us, are largely unable to comprehend what fate just might have in store for them. The cows may well be completely oblivious to what's going on—until the last moment. As for us, though, we know that something is afoot. Or some of us do. The problem, though, is that we cannot see the full scope of things. We are somewhat aware that there is a curtain of secrecy, but it's one that we are not fully able to penetrate to see what it hides. All we get are frustratingly brief glimpses of the other worlds and realms around us—which usually occur when the entities themselves intrude upon our world, rather than the other way around. Or, we dismiss the entire issue of supernatural ingestion as complete nonsense, the stuff of legend, folklore, bad dreams, and not much more else.

This denial, dismissal, and ignorance of the agenda of the paranormal parasites has allowed these things to operate in our world. This gives them carte blanche to do whatever they want, when they want, and how they want. As it once was millennia ago, when the likes of Lilith and the incubus instilled worldwide fear and fed on people, so it still is today, centuries later.

There is another important thing to note: There are strong indications that, despite the undeniable differences between some of these parasitic things, they also have deep similarities. This prompts the idea that many of them are semiconnected parts of a greater, mysterious whole. As we have seen, many of the attacks and assaults made on us—as a means to secure energy-based food—occur at night, when the targeted victim is asleep. The Shadow People, the incubus, the succubus, and the hungry ghost all typically attack in the early hours of the morning, which suggests a link between them all. This clearly cannot be a matter of coincidence and nothing else. What we are seeing is all of these things surfacing from their otherworldly lairs and feasting on us when we are our most vulnerable: while we are asleep.

There are other similarities too. When people are confronted by these terrible things, they fall sick—sometimes incredibly quickly. The Black-Eyed Children, the Shadow People, the djinn, the Men in Black, and the hungry ghost all look significantly different when it comes to the matter of their gruesome physical appearances. Yet the fact that all of them can cause the spontaneous development of severe ill health strongly suggests another high degree of commonality. Maybe they are one and the very same thing—manifesting in radically different forms for different eras, cultures, and countries. It's perhaps worth musing on the possibility that we have *never* seen the paranormal parasites in their true forms—only the guises they take on when they coldheartedly interact with us.

Let's now take a look at the angle of soul stealing in relation to the UFO phenomenon and the dwarfish Greys. Here we see evidence that even if we, the public, aren't getting the full story, certain elements of the US government may know what's going down. Or, probably more likely, they strongly suspect why we exist and what our fates could amount to. The references in highly classified files to the human race as "containers" of souls are as ominous as they are chillingly thought-provoking. The possibility that when we die our souls are somehow converted into the equivalent of a form of energy-based food is enough to give anyone nightmares. Huge, unending, hellish factories in which human souls are devoured? Good luck expecting the government to come clean on that one.

Many UFO researchers are highly critical of government agencies for hiding the truth from the public and the media. I say, try putting yourself in the position of those who are sitting on this terrible, earth-shattering secret. One can hardly blame them for not wanting to release a story that would, at the very least, be paradigm-destroying on a worldwide scale. So, the only thing they can do is to bury the entire issue as deeply as possible. There may well be a sense of "what the people don't know won't hurt them." Until the day arrives when it *does* hurt them, of course.

The secrecy surrounding UFOs may also exist to hide what is possibly going on far below the New Mexican town of Dulce. Yes, the tales of massive numbers of people kidnapped against their wills, harvested, and fed to hungry aliens are extremely controversial. As is the story told to the late Leonard

Stringfield of aliens acting like crazed butchers during the Vietnam War in 1972. If only a handful of such cases had occurred, that would be reason enough to hide the almost unbelievable truth. But multiply that figure by maybe thousands, or even tens of thousands, and it's no wonder that no one on the inside wants to talk about this. They don't know how to.

Then there are those extremely alternative parasites that we ourselves have created—thought-forms or tulpas. It's one thing to be attacked by a monster from another plane of existence and drained of our life forces. It's quite another, though, to fall victim to a creature that we ourselves have created. Richard Freeman's goal to manifest a tulpa version of Clark Ashton Smith's fictional spider-deity, Atlach-Nacha, is a perfect example. That Freeman succeeded in his goal was not a cause for celebration, though: it quickly became obvious to Freeman and his college friends that the monster was briefly and dangerously real—sucking in and gaining strength from their beliefs like a sponge in water.

It has to be said, though, that both examples are massively eclipsed by the phenomenal rise of the Slenderman, who began "life" as an internet-based character, but is now the ultimate tulpa. He is allowed to live as a result of the millions of kids and teenagers who hang on every word, every online story, every chat room message, and every movie that has the skinny monster at its heart. In a very strange way, by creating this particular breed of parasite, we are in essence eating ourselves. It's like a skewed, supernatural equivalent of *Soylent Green*.

It's important, too, to note that many of the so-called cryptids of our world—the Chupacabra and Bigfoot in particular—may not be all that they appear to be. The evidence shown in the pages of this book demonstrates that while at first glance these creatures might be perceived as just unknown animals, when we look a bit closer we see they are something else entirely.

The Chupacabra is, apparently, a monster that can be invoked by human blood, which energizes the deadly beast and gives it a greater foothold in our world. Bigfoot, meanwhile, utilizes the likes of infrasound, invisibility, and mind control, and may have found the perfect food supply in the many people who vanish from the national forests of the United States on a disturbingly regular basis, never to be seen again.

So where does all of this leave us? Are we all destined to be the food of vile, nonhuman creatures that have always been with us and may never go away? Is it our fate to become the nourishment of something else? We shouldn't be so surprised or dismissive of such a bleak scenario. After all, isn't that what most of us (vegetarians and vegans aside) do every day of every week of every year—namely, eat something else? Yes, it is. When we have a craving for a juicy steak, when we eat our Thanksgiving turkey, or when we dine on a plate of fajitas, do we give much thought to the source of the meal? For the most part, no, we don't.

It is, perhaps, our arrogance and our egos that lead us to believe we are at the top of the food chain. In reality, though, we may amount to a minor, collective link in that very same chain.

Charles Fort just might have been right on target when he said, "I think we're property."

BIBLIOGRAPHY

All websites without publication dates were accessed by the author in 2017.

One: Supernatural Energy

"A Brief History of Wilhelm Reich's Discoveries, and the Developing Science of Orgonomy." Orgone Biophysical Research Lab. Updated 1996. http://www.orgonelab.org/wrhistory.htm.

Chambers, Dr. Paul. *Sex & the Paranormal*. London: Blandford, 1999.

Denicola, Mark. "Understanding the Life Force Energy That Charges Us All: Orgone Energy & The Orgone Accumulator." Collective Evolution. Updated December 15, 2013. http://www.collective-evolution.com/2013/12/15/understanding-the-life-force-energy-that-charges-us-all-orgone-energy-the-orgone-accumulator/.

"Prana." Yoga in Daily Life. http://www.yogaindailylife.org/system/en/the-spiritual-background/prana.

"Prana: the Universal Life Force." Yoga: Magazine of the Bihar School of Yoga. Published 1982. http://www.yogamag.net/archives/1982/emay82/prana582.shtml.

"September 2008 Update From The Wilhelm Reich Infant Trust & The Wilhelm Reich Museum." Wilhelm Reich Infant Trust. Published September 2008. http://www.wilhelmreichtrust.org/update_08_09.html.

Shankar, Sri Sri Ravi. "What is Prana or Life force energy?" *Wisdom by Sri Sri Ravi Shankar* (blog). 2016. http://www.wisdom.srisriravishankar.org/what-is-prana-life-force-energy/.

"Wilhelm Reich." American College of Orgonomy. http://www.orgonomy.org/reich.html.

"Wilhelm Reich: Federal Bureau of Investigation." Archive. https://archive.org/details/WilhelmReichFBI.

Two: Lovers' Lane Beasts

Coleman, Loren. *Bigfoot!: The True Story of Apes in America*. New York: Paraview Pocket Books, 2003.

Downes, Jonathan. *Monster Hunter*. Woolsery, England: CFZ Press, 2004.

Gerhard, Ken. *Encounters with Flying Humanoids: Mothman, Manbirds, Gargoyles & Other Winged Beasts*. Woodbury, MN: Llewellyn Publications, 2013.

Hardy, Michael. "Bigfoot Is Hiding in the Big Thicket." *Houstonia*. April 30, 2014. https://www.houstoniamag.com/articles/2014/4/30/bigfoot-hiding-big-thicket-east-texas-may-2014.

Hometown. "Goatman's Summer of Celebrity (part 1): The Glamour Boy Of Greer Island." *Hometown by Handlebar* (blog). July 10, 2017. http://hometownbyhandlebar.com/?p=23098.

Hughes Babb, Christina. "Cat killings in Dallas continue." *Advocate Lakewood/East Dallas*. July 17, 2008. https://lakewood.advocatemag.com/2008/07/17/cat-killings-in-dallas-continue/.

Keel, John. *The Mothman Prophecies*. New York: Tor, 1991.

Riggs, Rob. *In the Big Thicket: On the Trail of the Wild Man*. New York: Paraview Press, 2001.

Shuker, Karl. "Sex and the Single Satyr." *Shukernature* (blog). August 9, 2012. http://karlshuker.blogspot.com/2012/08/sex-and-single-satyr.html.

Vaughn, Chris. "Mystery Still Engulfs Lake Worth Monster." NBC 5 Dallas-Fort Worth. August 8, 2009. http://www.nbcdfw.com/news/local/Mystery-Still-Engulfs-Lake-Worth-Monster-52597122.html.

Wamsley, Jeff. *Mothman: Behind the Red Eyes*. Point Pleasant: Mothman Press, 2005.

Wilonsky, Robert. "Dallas PD, SPCA Notice 'Disturbing Trend' in Cat Killings; Offer Reward in the Latest Case." *Dallas Observer*, April 14, 2011. http://www.dallasobserver.com/news/dallas-pd-spca-notice-disturbing-trend-in-cat-killings-offer-reward-in-the-latest-case-7103608.

Three: Black-Eyed Children

Cliff. "Brian Bethel—The Black Eyed Kids." *Pararational* (blog). May 16, 2013. https://pararational.com/brian-bethel-the-black-eyed-kids/.

Harold, Jim. "Can We Come In?—The Lore of the Black Eyed Children—Ryan Sprague's Hidden Auditorium." *The Paranormal Podcast*. October 27, 2015. http://jimharold.com/can-we-come-in-the-lore-of-the-black-eyed-children-ryan-spragues-hidden-auditorium/.

Weatherly, David. *The Black Eyed Children*. Denton, TX: Leprechaun Press, 2012.

Four: Shadow People

Hollis, Heidi. *The Hat Man: The True Story of Evil Encounters*. Milwaukee, WI: Level Head Publishing, 2014.

Offutt, Jason. *Darkness Walks: The Shadow People Among Us*. San Antonio, TX: Anomalist Books, 2009.

Five: Hungry Ghosts

Ankerberg, John, Dillon Burroughs, and John Weldon. "What Are the Pagan Roots of Halloween?" CBN. Accessed 2017. https://www1.cbn.com/the-pagan-roots-of-halloween.

"Chi: Universal Life Force Energy." Chi Machine International. *SOQI News Magazine.* Accessed 2017. http://www.chimachine4u.com/chi.html.

Heaphy, Linda. "Hungry Ghosts: Their History and Origin." *Kashgar* (blog). March 22, 2017. https://kashgar.com.au/blogs/tribal-culture/hungry-ghosts-their-history-and-origin.

"History of Halloween." History. Published 2009. http://www.history.com/topics/halloween/history-of-halloween.

"Jikininki." Yokai. Published 2016. http://yokai.com/jikininki/.

Sadhguru. "The Meaning of Karma and How You Can Break Its Grip." *Isha* (blog). December 25, 2012. http://isha.sadhguru.org/blog/yoga-meditation/is-my-karma-good-or-bad/.

Semaan, Jessica. "The hungry ghost and always wanting more." Medium. February 10, 2017. https://medium.com/@jessicasemaan/the-hungry-ghost-and-always-wanting-more-2bb397dbdc10.

Six: Bloodsuckers

"1975, February~July: The Vampire of Moca." Anomalies. Accessed 2017. http://anomalyinfo.com/Stories/1975-vampire-moca.

Arnold, Neil. *Paranormal London.* Stroud, England: The History Press, 2010.

Berard, Cyprien. *The Vampire Lord Ruthwen*. Tarzana, CA: Hollywood Comics, 2011.

Farrant, David. *Beyond the Highgate Vampire*. London: British Psychic and Occult Society, 1997.

"Gello." SuperNatural Creatures. Accessed 2017. http://supernaturalcreatures.org/encyclopedia/gello/.

"Highgate Vampire, London, England." Ghost Story. Accessed 2017. http://www.ghost-story.co.uk/index.php/unclassified/126-highgate-vampire-london-england.

McCabe, Joseph. *The Story of Religious Controversy*. Boston: Stratford Company, 1929.

McWilliams, Redmond. "Elizabeth Siddal—The First 'Vampire' of Highgate?" *The Vampire Exhumed!* (blog). February 7, 2013. http://thehighgatevampireexhumed.blogspot.com/2013/02/elizabeth-siddal-true-vampire-of.html.

Mingren, Wu. "Jure Grando and the First Documented Case of Vampirism in Europe." Ancient Origins. September 13, 2016. http://www.ancient-origins.net/myths-legends/jure-grando-and-first-documented-case-vampirism-europe-006640.

Offutt, Jason. "Revisiting the Highgate Vampire." Mysterious Universe. May 29, 2013. http://mysteriousuniverse.org/2013/05/revisiting-the-highgate-vampire/.

"Panteon de Belen Haunted Cemetery Legends." Explore Guadalajara. http://www.explore-guadalajara.com/hauntedcemetery.html.

Pina, Stephanie Graham. "About Elizabeth Siddal." *Exploring Elizabeth Siddal* (blog). Published 2004. http://lizziesiddal.com/portal/about-elizabeth-siddal/.

Polidori, John. *The Vampyre*. London: Henry Colburn, 1819.

Rymer, James Malcolm. *Varney the Vampire; or, The Feast of Blood*. Camarillo, CA: Zittaw Press, 2007.

Steiger, Brad. *Real Vampires, Night Stalkers and Creatures from the Darkside*. Detroit: Visible Ink Press, 2010.

Stoker, Bram. *Dracula*. Sweden, MI: Wisehouse Classics, 2016.

Swope, Robin. "The Vampire's Ghost of Guadalajara." *The Paranormal Pastor* (blog). August 21, 2008. http://theparanormalpastor.blogspot.com/2008/08/vampires-ghost-of-guadalajara.html.

"Vetala; possessing dead bodies!" Vampires.com. Accessed 2017. https://www.vampires.com/vetala-possessing-dead-bodies/.

"The Walking Dead: *draugr* and Aptrgangr in Old Norse Literature." The Viking Answer Lady. http://www.vikinganswerlady.com/ghosts.shtml.

Wright, Dudley. *The Book of Vampires*. New York: Causeway Books, 1973.

Seven: Mind Monsters

McGrath, Jim. "Conjuring Constantine." *The Laughing Magician* (blog). August 20, 2012. https://thelaughingmagician.wordpress.com/2012/08/20/conjuring-constantine/.

Nicholson, Andrew. "Poltergeists: Teen Angst & Telekinesis." Mysterious Universe. Updated November 13, 2012. http://mysteriousuniverse.org/2012/11/poltergeists-teen-angst-telekinesis/

"Poltergeists." Crystalinks. http://www.crystalinks.com/poltergeists.html.

Redfern, Nick. "Creating a Monstrous Mind-Spider." Mysterious Universe. August 19, 2015. http://mysteriousuniverse.org/2015/08/creating-a-monstrous-mind-spider/.

"Slender Man." The Slender Man Wiki. Accessed 2017. http://theslenderman.wikia.com/wiki/Slender_Man.

Smith, Clark Ashton. "The Seven Geases." *The Eldritch Dark* (blog). January 30, 2007. http://www.eldritchdark.com/writings/short-stories/192/the-seven-geases.

"Tulpa." *TV Tropes* (blog). Accessed 2017. http://tvtropes.org/pmwiki/pmwiki.php/Main/Tulpa.

"The Tulpa Effect." The Slender Man Wiki. Accessed 2017. http://theslenderman.wikia.com/wiki/The_Tulpa_Effect.

Eight: The Djinn

Emspak, Jesse. "States of Matter: Plasma." LiveScience. May 5, 2016. http://www.livescience.com/54652-plasma.html.

Guiley, Rosemary Ellen. *The Djinn Connection: The Hidden Links Between Djinn, Shadow People, ETs, Nephilim, Archons, Reptilians and Other Entities*. Pensacola: Visionary Living, Inc., 2013.

———. "A Short Course on the Djinn." Djinn Universe. 2016. http://www.djinnuniverse.com/a-short-course-on-the-djinn. Article no longer available online.

Guiley, Rosemary Ellen, and Philip J. Imbrogno. *The Vengeful Djinn: Unveiling the Hidden Agenda of Genies*. Woodbury, MN: Llewellyn Publications, 2011.

"Plasma: The Fourth State of Matter." Southwest Research Institute. Accessed 2017. http://pluto.space.swri.edu/image/glossary/plasma.html.

"What is plasma?" Qualitative Reasoning Group. Accessed 2017. http://www.qrg.northwestern.edu/projects/vss/docs/propulsion/2-what-is-plasma.html.

Williams, Matt. "A universe of 10 dimensions." Phys.org. December 11, 2014. https://phys.org/news/2014-12-universe-dimensions.html.

Nine: Soul Stealers

"Captain Lawrence Coyne UFO Helicopter case 1973." The Living Moon. Accessed 2017. http://www.thelivingmoon.com/49ufo_files/03files2/1973_Lawrence_Coyne_UFO_Helicopter_Case.html.

"Father Paul." *Telegraph*, June 28, 2010. http://www.telegraph.co.uk/news/obituaries/military-obituaries/naval-obituaries/7859545/Father-Paul.html.

Fort, Charles. *The Book of the Damned: The Collected Works of Charles Fort*. New York: Penguin Group, 2008.

Fuller, John G. *The Interrupted Journey*. New York: The Dial Press, 1966.

Henderson, Paul W. Document, September 21, 1961.

Hopkins, Budd. *Missing Time*. New York: Ballantine Books, 1981.

Inglesby, Paul. *UFOs and the Christian*. London: Regency Press, 1978.

Jacobsen, Annie. *Area 51: An Uncensored History of America's Top Secret Military Base*. New York: Little, Brown and Company, 2011.

Kerner, Nigel. *Grey Aliens and the Harvesting of Souls: The Conspiracy to Genetically Tamper with Humanity*. Rochester, VT: Bear & Company, 2010.

———. *The Song of the Greys*. London: Hodder and Stoughton, 1997.

Lindemann, Michael, ed. *UFOs and the Alien Presence: Six Viewpoints*. Columbus: Granite Publishing, 1995.

Mack, John E. *Abduction: Human Encounters with Aliens*. New York: Ballantine Books, 1995.

———. *Passport to the Cosmos: Human Transformation and Alien Encounters*. New York: Three Rivers Press, 2000.

Mair, Chris. "Obituary: Paul Inglesby." *The Scotsman*, July 5, 2010. http://www.scotsman.com/news/obituaries/obituary-paul-inglesby-1-816243.

Redfern, Nick. "Demons and the Defense Department." Mysterious Universe. June 4, 2015. http://mysteriousuniverse.org/2015/06/demons-and-the-defense-department/.

———. "Demons, Souls, *The Matrix*, and the Pentagon." Mysterious Universe. March 1, 2013. http://mysteriousuniverse.org/2013/03/demons-souls-the-matrix-and-the-pentagon/.

Strieber, Whitley. *Communion: A True Story*. New York: William Morrow Books, 1987.

———. *Transformation: The Breakthrough*. New York: William Morrow Books, 1988.

Ten: Aliens and Abductions

"2016 NCIC Missing Person and Unidentified Person Statistics." Federal Bureau of Investigation. https://www.fbi.gov/file-repository/2016-ncic-missing-person-and-unidentified-person-statistics.pdf/view.

"Animal Mutilation." The Vault. https://vault.fbi.gov/Animal%20Mutilation.

Bishop, Greg. *Project Beta: The Story of Paul Bennewitz, National Security, and the Creation of a Modern UFO Myth*. New York: Paraview Pocket Books, 2005.

Bishop, Jason, III. "The Dulce Base." Sacred Texts. http://www.sacred-texts.com/ufo/dulce.htm.

Bowman, Ben, ed. "The Alleged Secret Underground Alien Base In Dulce, New Mexico." Curiosity Makes You Smarter. August 11, 2016. https://curiosity.com/topics/the-alleged-secret-underground-alien-base-in-dulce-new-mexico-curiosity/.

Branton. "The Dulce Book." Whale. http://www.whale.to/b/dulce_b.html.

Bryant, Charles W. "What was Operation Plowshare?" How Stuff Works. April 28, 2016. http://www.stuffyoushouldknow.com/podcasts/what-was-operation-plowshare.htm.

Corso, Philip J., and William J. Birnes. *The Day After Roswell*. New York: Simon & Schuster, 1997.

Cutchin, Joshua. *A Trojan Feast: The Food and Drink Offerings of Aliens, Faeries, and Sasquatch*. San Antonio, TX: Anomalist Books, 2015.

Jacobs, David. *The Threat: Revealing the Secret Alien Agenda*. New York: Simon & Schuster, 1998.

Monaghan, Patricia. *The Encyclopedia of Celtic Mythology and Folklore*. New York: Checkmark Books, 2008.

"Project Gasbuggy Atomic Explosion Site." RoadsideAmerica. Accessed 2017. http://www.roadsideamerica.com/story/16912.

Stringfield, Leonard. *UFO Crash Retrievals: The Inner Sanctum*. Self-published, 1991.

Valerian, Valdamar. *Matrix II*. Yelm, WA: Leading Edge Research, 1990.

Eleven: Creatures That Make Us Sick

"Anorexia: Overview and Statistics." National Eating Disorders Association. https://www.nationaleatingdisorders.org/anorexia-nervosa.

McCabe, Joseph. *The Story of Religious Controversy*. Boston: The Stratford Company, 1929.

McClure, Kelly. "Salt Can Protect You From Evil and Make You Feel Calmer." The Hauntist. March 19, 2017. http://www.destinationamerica.com/thehauntist/how-to-protect-your-home-from-evil-spirits-using-salt/.

Redfern, Nick. *Men in Black*. Bracey, VA: Lisa Hagan Books, 2015.

Snow, Isabella. "How To Use A Smudge Stick." Exemplore. July 23, 2016. https://exemplore.com/misc/How-To-Use-A-Smudge-Stick.

"Understanding Anemia—the Basics." WebMD. Accessed 2017. http://www.webmd.com/a-to-z-guides/understanding-anemia-basics#1.

Twelve: Bedroom Invaders

Bible. New International Version. Colorado Springs, CO: Biblica, 2011. https://www.biblica.com/bible.

Carus, Paul. *The History of the Devil and the Idea of Evil*. Whitefish, MT: Kessinger Publishing, LLC, 2004.

"Encyclopedia Judaica: Alphabet of Ben Sira." Jewish Virtual Library. Accessed 2017. http://www.jewishvirtuallibrary.org/alphabet-of-ben-sira.

Erik. "What is a Succubus and Incubus Spirit." SuccuSummon. Updated 2012. http://www.summoningsuccubus.com/what-is-a-succubus-and-incubus-spirit/.

Knight, Kevin. "Whether the angels have bodies naturally united to them?" New Advent. http://www.newadvent.org/summa/1051.htm.

Kramer, Heinrich and James Sprenger. *Malleus Maleficarum*. Translated by Rev. Montague Summers. London: John Rodker, 1928. Electronic reproduction by Wicasta Lovelace and Christie Jury, 2000. http://www.malleusmaleficarum.org/.

"Popobawa." Occultopedia. Accessed 2017. http://www.occultopedia.com/p/popobawa.htm.

Schwarz, Rob. "The Old Hag Syndrome." Stranger Dimensions. October 13, 2011. https://www.strangerdimensions.com/2011/10/13/the-old-hag-syndrome/.

"The story of the African Tokoloshe." All Explore—Travel the World. Accessed 2017. http://www.allexplore.com/id906.htm.

Thompson, Reginald Campbell. *Devils and Evil Spirits of Babylonia*. Whitefish, MT: Kessinger Publishing, 2003.

Turner, Rebecca. "How to Stop Sleep Paralysis—and Transform it into a Lucid Dream." World of Lucid Dreaming. Accessed 2017. http://www.world-of-lucid-dreaming.com/sleep-paralysis.html.

Weatherly, David. *Strange Intruders*. Nevada: Leprechaun Productions, 2011.

Thirteen: Monsters of a Mysterious Island

Hill, Bryan. "The Legend of the Fearsome Chupacabra in Puerto Rico." Ancient Origins. August 30, 2015. http://www.ancient-origins.net/myths-legends-americas/legend-fearsome-chupacabra-puerto-rico-003706.

"Puerto Rican Chupacabra." Cryptid Wiki. Accessed 2017. http://cryptidz.wikia.com/wiki/Puerto_Rican_Chupacabra.

Redfern, Nick. *Chupacabra Road Trip*. Woodbury, MN: Llewellyn Publications, 2015.

Fourteen: Bigfoot

"2017 NCIC Missing Person and Unidentified Person Statistics." FBI. Published 2017. https://www.fbi.gov/file-repository/2017-ncic-missing-person-and-unidentified-person-statistics.pdf/view/.

Barackman, Cliff. "A Case for Infrasound." CliffBarackman.com. Published 2013. http://cliffbarackman.com/research/articles-2/a-case-for-infrasound/.

Coleman, Loren. *Bigfoot!: The True Story of Apes in America*. New York: Paraview Pocket Books, 2003.

Ghose, Tia. "Why Earth's Largest Ape Went Extinct." Live Science. January 11, 2016. https://www.livescience.com/53313-biggest-ape-forest-dweller.html.

Haas, George. *Bigfoot Bulletin*. October 31, 1970.

Merrick, Elliott. *True North: A Journey into Unexplored Wilderness*. Berkeley, CA: North Atlantic Books, 2010.

"Missing 411." North America Bigfoot Search. http://www.nabigfootsearch.com/missing_411.html.

Roosevelt, Theodore. *The Wilderness Hunter*. New York: G. B. Putnam's Sons, 1893.

Swancer, Brent. "Some Very Strange Information on the Bizarre Vanishing of Dennis Martin." Mysterious Universe. June 9, 2017. http://mysteriousuniverse.org/2017/06/some-very-strange-information-on-the-bizarre-vanishing-of-dennis-martin/.

Weidenreich, Franz. *Apes, Giants, and Man*. Chicago: University of Chicago Press, 1946.

Fifteen: Zombies

"Aswang." Cryptid Wiki. http://cryptidz.wikia.com/wiki/Aswang.

Chris. "The Kikiyaon Monster." *Real Unexplained Mysteries* (blog). August 22, 2014. http://realunexplainedmysteries.com/the-kikiyaon-monster.

Prof. Geller. "Aswang." Mythology.net. http://mythology.net/monsters/aswang/.

Merriam-Webster. s.v. "Ghoul," Accessed 2017. https://www.merriam-webster.com/dictionary/ghoul.

Green, Nadege, and Audra D. S. Burch, "The unraveling of Rudy Eugene, aka, the causeway face attacker." *Miami Herald*, July 14, 2012. http://www.miamiherald.com/news/special-reports/causeway-attack/article1941239.html.

"The Wendigo Legend." Gods and Monsters. 2016. http://www.gods-and-monsters.com/wendigo-legend.html.

Sixteen: Energy Suckers

Arnold, Kenneth & Ray Palmer. *The Coming of the Saucers*. Amherst: Legend Press, 1996.

Arnold, Neil. *Paranormal London*. Stroud, England: The History Press, 2010.

Barker, Gray. *They Knew Too Much About Flying Saucers*. Point Pleasant, WV: New Saucerian Books, 1967.

Bender, Albert K. *Flying Saucers and the Three Men*. New York: Paperback Library, Inc., 1968.

Keel, John A. *The Mothman Prophecies: A True Story*. New York: Tom Doherty Assosicates, LLC., 2002.

Keel. John A. *Operation Trojan Horse: The Classic Breakthrough Study of UFOs*. London: Abacus, 1973.

Keel, John A. *Visitors from Space*. St. Albans, England: Granada Publishing, Ltd., 1976.

Koch, Jo Ann. *Aliens, Abductions and Other Curious Encounters*. Self-published, 2015.

Marden, Kathleen, and Denise Stoner. *The Alien Abduction Files: The Most Startling Cases of Human Alien Contact Ever Reported*. Pompton Plains, NJ: The Career Press, Inc., 2013.

Medway, Gareth J. "Men in Black Encounters, a Short Catalogue." *Magonia* (blog). http://pelicanist.blogspot.com/p/mib-encounters.html.

Redfern, Nick. *Men in Black*. Bracey, VA: Lisa Hagan Books, 2015.

Redfern, Nick. *The Real Men in Black: Evidence, Famous Cases, and True Stories of These Mysterious Men and their Connection to UFO Phenomena*. Pompton Plains, NJ: New Page Books, 2011.

Redfern, Nick. *Women in Black*. Bracey, VA: Lisa Hagan Books, 2016.

Sutherly, Curt. *UFO Mysteries: A Reporter Seeks the Truth*. Woodbury, MN: Llewellyn Publications, 2001.

Weatherly, David. "Children of the Men in Black." Contained in Nick Redfern's book, *Men in Black*. Bracey, VA: Lisa Hagan Books, 2015.

ACKNOWLEDGMENTS

A very big "thank you!" goes out to all of the following: Everyone at Llewellyn Publications, and particularly Amy Glaser, Kevin Brown, Annie Burdick, Kat Sanborn, and Bob Gaul. My literary agent, Lisa Hagan, for her hard work, enthusiasm, and friendship. And, of course, many thanks to everyone who generously shared their accounts of paranormal parasites with me.

Photo by Shane Van Boxtel

About the Author

Nick Redfern is the author of more than forty books on the worlds of the paranormal, the supernatural, and the unknown. His previous titles include *Chupacabra Road Trip*, *Shapeshifters*, *Nessie*, and *Men in Black*. Nick has appeared on dozens of television shows, including Syfy channel's *Proof Positive*, History channel's *Monster Quest*, and Nat Geo Wild's *The Monster Project*. He lives just a short drive from the infamous Grassy Knoll of Dallas, Texas. Nick can be contacted at his blog, *World of Whatever*: http://nickredfernfortean.blogspot.com.